the Big Grill

the Big Grill

Paul Kirk

CASSELL ILLUSTRATED

A QUINTET BOOK

First published in Great Britain in 2003 by Cassell Illustrated
a Member of Octopus Publishing Group Limited
2-4 Heron Quays, London E14 4JP

A CIP catalogue record for this book is available from the British Library.

ISBN 1 84403 099 7

This book was designed and produced by
Quintet Publishing Limited
6 Blundell Street
London N7 9BH

Photography Juliet Piddington
Food stylist Kathryn Hawkins
Art direction and Design Simon Daley
Editor Erin Connell

Managing Editor Diana Steedman
Creative Director Richard Dewing
Publisher Oliver Salzmann

Manufactured in Singapore by Universal Graphics
Printed in China by Leefung-Asco Printers Trading Ltd

Contents

BARBECUE BASICS   1

A short history of barbecuing

How barbecuing actually started is unknown. I would venture to guess that an unfortunate animal got caught in a volcanic eruption or fell into a fire pit, and a man came along and pulled it out, accidentally ending up with some of the hot flesh on his hands. He licked his hand, liked what he tasted and never looked back. That's only one theory – there are many others – but what is known is that people have been cooking over coals since the beginning of time. Ancient barbecue pits have been unearthed during archeological digs in China and, more recently, in Spain, where a 150,000-year-old pit was unearthed. The existence of fire pits to cook meats has been dated as far back as 2500 BC. The writings of Homer suggest that the Greeks were preparing oxen, sheep and swine in an open grill or fire pit long before the birth of Christ. Homer tells us that Achilles prepared a meal for Ajax, Odysseus and Phoenix in which a sheep, a goat and a pig were butchered and salted, then grilled over live coals. But how did we get the name barbecue? Early Spanish explorers came to the New World and found the Native Americans cooking their meat on sticks and on grills, which they called *barbacoa* – which was translated to the word barbecue that we use today.

A world of barbecues

Barbecue as we know it today has enjoyed a boom in popularity during the last several decades, not only in the United States, Australia and Europe, but all over the globe. The oldest cooking method known is still being practised and with delicious results. Here is a brief tour of barbecuing and grilling around the world.

In South Korea, you may enjoy *bulgogi* – thin strips of beef marinated in soy sauce, rice wine and seasonings. The meat and accompaniments are brought to you to cook the meal yourself over a grill in the centre of the table. The grill is shaped like a hubcap, has a brass grill-top and is fuelled with bamboo charcoal. You cook the meat to the desired doneness, wrap it in a green leaf lettuce or sesame leaf, and top it with kimchee (a fiery hot sauce made with cabbage, garlic and onions). It is truly delightful.

In Japan, there are many different grilling techniques. In restaurants, the customer cooks teriyaki chicken and beef kebabs over a grill set into the middle of the table. Prawns (shrimp), squid (calamari) and yakitori (marinated chicken and leeks on skewers) are often cooked outdoors on a Japanese barbecue or *hibachi*. People may go to yakitori stands, which are very basic affairs – perhaps six stools pushed against a counter that houses the *hibachi*. The succulent skewers are dipped in a sauce and then grilled to perfection, usually washed down with a cold beer. Okonomiyaki shops, which are very popular with students, involve cooking your own vegetable-filled pancake on a charcoal-fired hot plate in the centre of the table.

A signature Indonesian grilled dish is *saté* – marinated cubes of meat, fish, or poultry threaded onto skewers and grilled over a hot fire. *Saté* is served with peanut and other sauces, using a recipe derived from the Arab spice traders.

The Thai people grill using bamboo- and coconut shell-charcoal. Their tangy and delicious marinades are based on lime juice, garlic, galangal, lemongrass and hot peppers. Basic charcoal grills are set up on the pavement to cook kebabs, fish and marinated chicken. The method is simple and the ingredients are often few, but the results are mind blowing.

In Brazil, restaurants serve whole joints of meat that have been grilled on large, sword-like skewers. The skewers are then brought to your table where a portion is carved off. Known as *churrasco*, it is both a great feast and a great spectacle.

Jerk is Jamaican barbecue and is a cooking method, a national dish and a way of life. Spicy and tasty, it is a blend of Scotch bonnet chilli peppers, allspice and lime juice or vinegar. Jamaican jerk has been traced back to the Arawak Indians, who are credited as one of the originators of barbecue.

The Argentinians grill in several ways. One way is by covering the ground with hot coals and staking a whole lamb or suckling pig into the ground, positioning it so it's angled towards the fire in order to cook slowly and succulently. The second way, which can be attributed to the Gauchos, is to grill small foods like sausages, mixed grill skewers, kidneys and other offal.

The Australians are barbecue aficionados, and at public beaches you find large, open bar grills that are available for anyone to use, making them great places to hold cook-outs. There is an abundance of fresh fish and shellfish, and "surf and turf" (fish and meat dishes) is popularly eaten together.

Turkish skewered meat or fish is known as *shish kebab*, while the large rotating tower of meat slowly grilling in traditional Turkish restaurants is called *doner*. The Greeks enjoy spit-cooked lamb or skewered lamb as *souvlakia*, as well as minced pork and herbs served as *kebabs*.

Countries and cultures that prepare their own version of barbecue are almost too numerous to list: in North Africa and the Middle East, grilled food is called *meshwi*; in Mali, street vendors sell *kyinkyinga*, a type of kebab; in France, you would be served *brochettes*; and tilapia, grilled over a smoky charcoal fire, is a common sight in African streets.

These are just some of the countries where grilling is a way of life – breakfast, lunch and dinner – all year round. As the motto of the Kansas City Barbecue Society goes, "Barbecue isn't just for breakfast anymore."

Getting fired up

Grilling is cooking food quickly over hot coals. Direct heat seals the food on the outside while the inside retains its tenderness and succulence. Barbecuing, traditionally, refers to cooking over indirect heat with the barbecue lid in place, as with a covered barbecue pit that allows heat to be conducted around the food, acting rather like an oven. This type of cooking is particularly suitable for whole chickens, legs of lamb and large, meaty fish. However, this book goes along with popular conception and

makes little distinction between barbecuing and grilling. Where food should be covered by the lid to achieve an indirect heat this is indicated in the recipe.

Buying a barbecue or grill

A grill is any vessel that can hold a fire and withstand heat. It can be a simple hole in the ground or an elaborate ceramic structure offering you a complete "outdoor kitchen". When buying a barbecue, you need to consider several factors, including the amount of money and space you have available, the type of fuel that you wish to use, how often you will use it and what you intend to cook on it. Outlined below are the most widely used types of fuel: charcoal, gas and electric.

Charcoal barbecues For many, a charcoal barbecue is the only way to cook, and there is nothing that can be said or done to persuade them otherwise. Purists say that cooking over charcoal is the best way to achieve that delicious, smoky flavour in your food. They find that the building, stoking and nurturing of the fire is part of the overall experience and tradition of barbecuing. Charcoal requires more judgement and skill to be operated effectively than do gas or electric.

Kettle, covered or hooded barbecues These three barbecues are similar, as they all feature a lid or cover. With the cover off, you can grill on an open rack; with the cover on, it is as though using a conventional oven because the heat circulates around the food. Either way, there is the additional bonus of imparting the aromas and flavours of open-fire cooking into your food. Kettle or hooded barbecues are particularly good for roasting because of their domed shape and the placement of air vents, and can add smoked flavours to foods if a handful of wood chips is added to the fire. And they are easy to store, easy to clean and are versatile enough to cook a range of foods.

Hibachi Literally meaning "fire bowl", these traditional Japanese charcoal-burners are comprised of a shallow, cast iron bowl for the fire, along with a series of notches that allow the cooking racks to be raised and lowered. The heavier, cast iron models are more effective because the thicker metal distributes the heat better than in the lighter, steel versions. They are inexpensive and portable, making them the ideal choice for beach barbecues and picnics.

Pedestal or pillar barbecues These slender grills are made up of a fire bowl set on a hollow tube that is stuffed with newspaper to help ignite the charcoal. When buying a pedestal grill, first consider its location in your garden, back yard or balcony because these grills need to have a very stable surface to stand on. They are easy to light, quick to reach cooking temperature and the ventilation holes allow you to control the rate at which the coals burn.

Disposable barbecues These are small, cheap and portable – perfect for picnics, the beach or for those barbecuing for the first time. They usually include a rack sitting over a foil tray of charcoal that has been impregnated with lighter fluid. They are easy to light, ready to use in 15 minutes and are perfectly suited to cooking smaller food such as burgers, kebabs and vegetables.

Homemade barbecues A brick-built barbecue on your patio makes barbecuing part of your everyday life. There are commercial kits available containing fireboxes, grids and racks that can be incorporated into a permanent or temporary brick structure. Homemade barbecues can be made from a range of materials, from a big metal drum to a flowerpot. My father's first barbecue grill was made from 36 cinder blocks and two metal grates he purchased from the junkyard for next to nothing. If you are seriously thinking about building your own barbecue, carefully consider its location. Avoid regularly used pathways, overhanging trees, children's play areas, and orientate the open side of the grill towards the prevailing breezes so that you can catch the draughts to keep the fire going.

Gas barbecues Gas barbecues are convenient and more easily controlled than charcoal barbecues, and they can be ready for use almost immediately. Available in a variety of sizes, from large trolleys to small, portable barbecues, the bottled or cylinder gas heats the lava rocks or flavouring plates that cook

Disposable barbecue

Fold-away grill

Bucket barbecue

the food. Gas barbecue addicts argue that the taste achieved by gas barbecues matches that produced by charcoal grills in a fraction of the time. A large gas barbecue is ideal for large parties or for those who want to mingle with their guests without keeping their eye on the fire!

Trolley barbecues Fast, easy to use and versatile the trolley barbecue is an all-around grill, with some models featuring three or four burners, a wok burner and a rotisserie. Often gas-powered, trolley barbecues can be expensive and require a lot of storage space because of their size. They are movable rather than portable, but are generally fuss-free and versatile enough to cook a range of foods.

Electric barbecues Available in a range of sizes, from the large trolley to the smaller, more portable versions, the electric grill offers the same advantages as the gas grill. Electric grills provide a good constant heat source but do not get as hot as charcoal. Another disadvantage of electric barbecues is that you have to be close to a power source or have an extension

cord long enough to reach the barbecue site. This must also involve taping down the electrical wires to ensure the safety of everyone in your party.

The right fuel

The success of a great barbecue is a great fire. Deciding on the best fuel-type for you will come with experimentation and experience. For minimum fuss, gas is likely to be your best choice. But if you enjoy the whole outdoor experience, then give charcoal a go. Whatever you choose, with a little practice and knowledge of technique, you will be cooking up a storm.

Lump or natural charcoal Made by burning hardwood without oxygen until all the impurities have been removed, the result is pure carbon – a black, glossy, lightweight product. Natural charcoal burns hotter and cleaner than charcoal

Kettle barbecue   *Pedestal grill*   *Trolley barbecue*

briquettes. Charcoal ignites quickly and burns fairly quickly for about 45 minutes, perfect for searing food while helping it retain its succulence.

Briquette charcoal Briquette charcoal, which is widely available, is made from compressed charcoal particles and is often impregnated with chemicals to help it ignite more easily. Briquette charcoal provides a consistent and steady heat and tends to burn longer than natural charcoal. Briquettes are also available made from pecan shells, bamboo and coconut husks, all of which burn hotter than domestic charcoal and impart their own unique flavours to the food.

Wood (logs, chunks, chips) With the wide availability of charcoal, wood-fire barbecuing is growing in popularity. Ensure that you know the source of the wood you are burning and don't burn wood treated with chemicals, or softwood such as pine which is full of resin. Use hardwood and fruit woods as below. If you are using charcoal, a handful of wood chips thrown on the hot coals will impart different flavours to your grill:

Hickory Pungent, smoky, bacon-like flavour

Oak Heavy smoke flavour

Apple Slightly sweet, but dense, fruity smoke flavour

Pecan Similar to oak but not as strong

Cherry Slightly sweet and fruity smoke flavour

Mesquite Strong, earthy flavours

Alder Delicate with a hint of sweetness

Maple Mild, smoky, sweet flavour.

Sure-fire tools and accessories

Before experiencing the thrill of the grill there are a few essential items that you need to be a flaming success.

Charcoal Chimney This is an inexpensive, cylindrical metal structure that can be set on the fire grate. Charcoal sits in the top section and crumpled newspaper in the bottom. It is handy for getting your fire going quickly and also helps to keep your fire supplied with hot coals. Start your extra coals in the chimney roughly 20 minutes before you need them.

Fire Starters Long stick matches are the obvious and safest choice, but there are many other methods of lighting up. Wax starters are long, fibrous sticks soaked with paraffin or beeswax to aid the lighting process. I prefer to use the small, wax-like cubes specifically designed for lighting barbecues. Kindling (such as wood shavings or small twigs) and paper are useful additions to the charcoal fire if placed underneath the charcoal before lighting. The paper will often allow the fire to "catch" the briquettes. An electric fire starter is a wand that you plug into an electrical outlet and it glows red hot to start your charcoal. Never use any form of lighter fuel that has not been specifically manufactured to light charcoal barbecues. Never use petroleum-based firelighters even though they are safe to use, as they give off an odour that can taint the food.

Long-handled Cooking Tools These include tongs, fish slices for turning, basting brushes, forks and skewers for testing doneness and spatulas for serving. Wooden-handled tools are best as they do not conduct heat as efficiently as metal.

Apron and Mitts Use a thick, non-flammable apron to protect your clothes and a good pair of heatproof mitts is essential.

Spritzing Bottles and Baking Soda A spritzing bottle of water and a carton of baking soda are useful items to douse the fire or control a flare-up. A second spritzing bottle containing basting liquid or apple juice is a good idea to keep the food moist and succulent.

Meat Thermometer If you are unsure of whether large joints of meat or whole chickens are cooked through, a meat thermometer measures the internal temperature.

Hinged Wire Grids or Grill Baskets These are available in various shapes and are designed to hold meat, fish or vegetables. Using a basket makes turning the food easier, but be sure to wear your heatproof mitts when handling it.

Metal and Bamboo Skewers Flat skewers are the best because they stop food from slipping as you turn it on the grill. Bamboo skewers need to be soaked in cold water for 30 minutes prior to cooking to help prevent them from simply burning away on the barbecue. They will still char, but remain intact.

Lighting up

Your grill should be sited on a solid, level ground away from low trees. A smaller grill such as an *hibachi* can be raised from the ground but should be securely placed on a heat-resistant surface. In the event of sudden wet weather, never be tempted to try and grill indoors!

When lighting up, make sure you are dressed sensibly in a protective apron and mitts and that children and animals are a safe distance away. Make sure you have everything you need before you start, as a burning grill should never be left unattended. Never light up in a high wind and always make sure that matches and lighter fuels are kept a safe distance away from the flame. In the event of a sudden flare-up, use your spritzer bottle of water or a handful of baking soda to douse the flames. In the (rare) event that a fire gets out of control, it is always useful to keep some sand handy to put out the flames.

Do not attempt to use charcoal in a gas grill. Check that the gas regulator is appropriate for your barbecue and that the connecting hoses and taps are in good working order. For electric grills, check the circuits and wires periodically and do not cook in wet weather.

From go to glow!

To light a charcoal barbecue, allow about 45 minutes before you want to start cooking. Remove the lid and open the vents wide. Spread charcoal briquettes, about two layers thick, across the base of the grill, piled into a neat heap in the centre. Alternatively, put the fuel into a charcoal chimney and light. Leave the coals for 10 minutes or so until they glow red, then spread them back over the base in an even layer using long-handled tongs. Leave them for another 25 to 30 minutes to heat up, waiting until the charcoal is ash grey before starting to cook.

To light a gas barbecue, allow about 10 minutes preheating. Open the lid and turn on the burners. Close the lid and allow the heat to reach the desired cooking temperature. Refer to your manufacturer's instructions for this, but generally, a gas barbecue takes 10 to 15 minutes to heat up.

Grilling techniques are not difficult to master. Basically, to be successful, it is a matter of paying attention to what you are doing and keeping a close eye on the food.

THE HAND TEST

Now, use the "hand test" to judge the heat of your grill. Hold your hand palm side down over the coals. If you can hold your hand steadily over the heat for no more than 2 seconds, you can judge the fire hot. See below for a rough guide to other grill temperatures.

Hot	**2 seconds**
Medium-hot	**3 seconds**
Medium	**4 seconds**
Medium-low	**5 seconds**
Low	**6 or more seconds**

If your fire has become too hot, and you're running too fast, don't despair – just turn the food more frequently. Covering the grill, and/or closing the air vents, are other ways to lower the heat. For example, if you were cooking a pork tenderloin and the recipe suggests turning it every 5 to 7 minutes, but the heat is too high to wait that long without burning, turn it every 3 minutes instead. If the coals lose their heat, or you wish to prolong cooking time, add fresh coals around the hot coals; placing them on top will kill the heat.

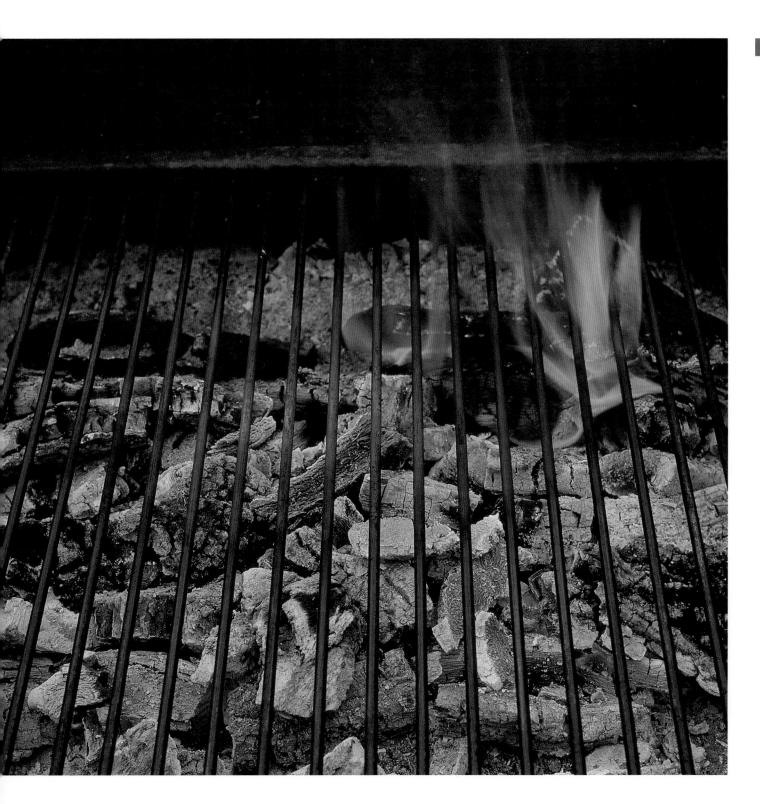

All-season grilling

Many people enjoy year-round grilling, so your grill need not be sent into hibernation for the winter months. According to one leading survey, nearly half of all Americans grill all year long, which includes the winter months. I will grill 365 days a year if need be, and I have even cooked when the wind-chill factor made it feel like -6ºC/21ºF. However, there are significant differences between barbecuing in warm and cold weathers, not least to ensure heavier clothing is kept clear of the heat.

Cooking in cold weather will necessitate using 10 to 20 per cent more fuel, depending upon how windy and cold it is. It will also increase your cooking times, sometimes considerably. This is because heat dissipates more quickly from your barbecue in cold weather than it does in warmer weather. One solution is to

insulate your grill using foil-backed insulation material. Securely wrap the foil around the bottom portion of the grill to insulate the firebox, and use a piece to help insulate the lid. Some barbecue manufacturers produce their own insulated covers to fit their designs, otherwise it could involve a bit of DIY!

Maintenance is important for your grill in the colder months. Before it gets cold, check your barbecue for efficiency, as grilling in cold weather puts more demands on your burners.

Keep your grill in a sheltered spot away from fences, low trees and other flammable structures. If you cannot do this, then grilling outdoors on a windy evening is not recommended.

Allow sufficient time for the grill to warm up, over and above the usual heating times. The colder it is, the longer it will take for your grill to heat up. To keep the temperature up, add some raw coals or raw wood to your charcoal fire during the cooking process. The addition of raw fuels to the fire will keep the flames fed and the temperatures high. Never, however, add raw fuels to your gas barbecue.

Always keep your barbecue covered while cooking and try to avoid the temptation to lift the lid too often. Don't ignore your food, of course, but by limiting the amount of times the lid is removed, your cooking will take less time and your steaks will be succulent and delicious.

Red hot maintenance

Oil your grill racks regularly so that food does not stick. Keep your grill as free from grease as possible. To clean it, scrub the grill racks with a wire brush or spatula before and after cooking. Clean the ashes from your firebox when they have cooled and dispose of them in a metal dustbin with a lid. Before storing the barbecue away for winter, use an oven cleaner to remove heavy, burnt-on deposits that have gathered on the grill grates.

Looking after your grill will make it last longer. At the end of the season, give all your tools a thorough cleaning, making sure to dry everything completely before storing it so that it doesn't rust. Try to store your barbecue away from the elements, or at the very least cover it properly with a waterproof covering.

MARINADES AND RUBS 2

Piri piri glaze

Piri piri is Portugal's favourite hot spicy sauce, and kicks this first section off with a powerful start!

3 hot red chillies, deseeded and chopped finely
3 tbsp olive oil
3 tbsp packed brown sugar
1 tbsp white wine vinegar
2 cloves garlic, crushed
1 tbsp tomato purée
125 ml/½ cup water

1 Place all the ingredients in a small pan. Bring to the boil. Simmer over low heat until the glaze thickens.

2 Remove from the heat and let cool.

Makes 175 ml/¾ cup

Barbecue mop

The proportion of vinegar may seem high in this recipe, but don't be put off by it, because it works well with fish, meat or vegetables.

6 tbsp cider vinegar
3 tbsp water
1½ tbsp Worcestershire sauce
1½ tbsp vegetable oil
2 tsp sea salt
2 tsp freshly ground black pepper
1½ tsp cayenne pepper

Combine the ingredients in a medium bowl. Brush over the food to be grilled before cooking, and then frequently during cooking.

Makes 125 ml/½ cup

Orange honey glaze

Although this recipe is simple to make and uses only three ingredients, it packs a huge flavour punch.

6 tbsp honey
Zest and juice of 1 orange
2 tbsp mirin (sweet rice wine)

1 Place the ingredients in a small saucepan. Bring to the boil. Boil vigorously until reduced by half.

2 Remove from the heat and let cool. Use for brushing over meat during the last 10 minutes of grilling.

Makes 125 ml/½ cup

Opposite Piri piri glaze

Cajun dry rub

Chefs from New Orleans helped popularise Cajun cuisine, including spice rubs like the one here. You can buy premixed spice mixes in the supermarket, but nothing is ever as good as homemade.

2 tbsp hot paprika

1 tbsp dried thyme

1 tbsp ground cumin

1 tbsp garlic powder

1 tbsp onion powder

1 tsp freshly ground black pepper

1 tsp sea salt

1 tsp cayenne pepper

1 tsp ground marjoram

Combine the ingredients in a small bowl and mix well.

Makes 50 g

How dow rub

An extraordinary name for a truly fiery rub to try on beef steaks or chicken.

1 tbsp dried mustard

3 tbsp hot paprika

1 tbsp onion powder

1 tbsp garlic powder

1 tbsp sea salt

1 tsp freshly ground black pepper

½ tsp bay leaf powder

Combine the ingredients in a small bowl and mix well.

Makes 50 g

Mango butter

If mangoes are unavailable, substitute 100 g each of peaches and pineapple purée, and use as directed.

225 g unsalted butter, softened

225 g fresh or jarred mango, peeled or drained and puréed

2 tsp lime juice

2 tbsp finely chopped fresh mint

1 tsp grated nutmeg

Mash the softened butter with a fork and add the remaining ingredients. Wrap the mixture in clingfilm and roll into the shape of a log. Refrigerate until needed.

Makes 1 cup

Above left Cajun dry rub **right** Mango butter

Green peppercorn butter

Pernod is a licorice-flavoured liqueur from France. If you don't have it on hand, you may substitute any other licorice- or anise-flavoured spirit.

1 tbsp green peppercorns preserved in brine, drained
100 g unsalted butter, softened
3 shallots, chopped finely
1 tsp Pernod

1 Crush the peppercorns using a mortar and pestle.

2 Combine with the remaining ingredients in a small bowl.

3 Wrap in clingfilm and roll into a log shape, about 2.5 cm in diameter. Refrigerate until needed.

Makes 100 g

Butter, lemon and herb marinade

To use, add to chicken, fish or meat and marinate at room temperature for 1 hour or brush on while grilling. You can use dried herbs instead of fresh, but be sure to reduce the amount of herbs by half.

100 g unsalted butter
Juice of 1 lemon
2 tbsp finely chopped, mixed fresh herbs, such as rosemary, thyme and marjoram
4 cloves garlic, chopped
Freshly ground black pepper

1 Gently melt the butter in a saucepan. Add the remaining ingredients and mix well.

2 Cover and marinate food at room temperature for 1 hour, or brush on while grilling.

Makes about 125 ml/¹⁄₂ cup

Honey and mustard marinade

If you like a little spice with your food, increase the dashes of cayenne pepper.

3 tbsp honey
1 tbsp dried mustard
3 tbsp olive oil
225 ml/1 cup pineapple juice
Juice of 1 orange
2 tbsp tomato purée
Dash of cayenne pepper
Freshly ground black pepper, to taste

1 Place the honey, mustard, oil, pineapple and orange juice, and tomato purée in a small saucepan and mix well. Bring to the boil and simmer for 15 minutes.

2 Stir in the cayenne and black pepper. Let cool before using.

Makes 350 ml/1¹⁄₂ cups

Opposite Green peppercorn butter

Balsamic vinegar herb marinade

These days, a well-stocked kitchen includes a bottle of balsamic vinegar, so this marinade should be easy to throw together. This is especially good on grilled vegetables.

6 tbsp olive oil

2 tbsp balsamic vinegar

2 spring onions (white and green parts), chopped finely

2 tbsp finely chopped parsley

1 tbsp finely chopped rosemary

1½ tsp finely chopped thyme

Sea salt and freshly ground black pepper, to taste

Combine all the ingredients in a small bowl and mix well.

Makes about 125 ml/½ cup

Chermoula

This marinade is a beautiful green colour due to the abundance of fresh coriander and parsley called for in the recipe.

1 bunch coriander, chopped finely

1 large bunch parsley, chopped finely

6 cloves garlic, crushed

1 tbsp ground cumin

1 tsp ground coriander

1 tbsp paprika

¼ tsp cayenne pepper

Juice of 2 lemons

300 ml/1¼ cups olive oil

Combine the dry ingredients in a large bowl and mix well. Add the lemon juice and oil and stir thoroughly.

Makes about 450 ml/2 cups

Opposite Chermoula

Sweet-and-sour marinade

The exotic ingredients required here give a hint to its origins in Indonesia. Most Asian markets will carry the shrimp paste and a selection of soy sauces.

1 tbsp cumin seeds	8 tbsp hot water
1 tbsp coriander seeds	3 tbsp sweet soy sauce
3 tbsp groundnut oil	3 tbsp lime juice
2 medium onions, peeled and chopped	1/4 tsp chilli powder
3 cloves garlic, peeled	Sea salt and freshly ground black pepper, to taste
3 tbsp shrimp paste	

1 Roast the cumin and coriander seeds in a heavy skillet until they start to colour, then grind using a mortar and pestle or electric coffee grinder. Set aside.

2 Heat the oil in a frying pan and, when hot, add the onions and garlic. Stir-fry until they begin to brown. Stir in the shrimp paste and continue to cook until it begins to brown. Place in a blender or food processor with the hot water and blend to a paste.

3 Put the paste into a bowl with the roasted spices, add the sweet soy sauce, lime juice, chilli powder, salt and pepper. Mix well.

Makes 225 ml/1 cup

Lemongrass and ginger marinade

This Southeast Asian-inspired marinade is especially delicious on chicken or pork. Galangal, also known as Thai ginger, is similar in flavour to "regular" ginger and can be found in Asian markets.

2 lemongrass stalks, inside soft part only, sliced finely	2 cloves garlic, chopped finely
5-cm piece root ginger, or galangal if available, peeled and chopped	2 tbsp groundnut oil
	2 tbsp fish sauce
2 to 4 Thai chillies, according to taste	2 tbsp packed brown sugar
	1 tbsp lime juice
1 red pepper, deseeded and chopped finely	4 tbsp water
1 medium onion, chopped finely	

Place the ingredients in a blender or food processor and blend to a smooth paste.

Makes 175 ml/³⁄₄ cup

Opposite Lemongrass and ginger marinade

Teriyaki red wine marinade

Teriyaki is a Japanese soy sauce that's very smooth and deep flavoured, making it ideal for marinating. In Japanese, *teri* means "sunshine" and *yaki* means "roast" or "grilled", so what could be more suitable for barbecuing? This marinade is particularly good with beef, lamb and duck.

4 tbsp Teriyaki sauce

4 tbsp red wine

1 tbsp sesame oil

1 tbsp finely chopped root ginger

2 large cloves garlic, chopped finely

Combine the ingredients in a medium bowl and mix well.

Makes 125 ml/½ cup

Coriander, lime and vermouth marinade

Dry white vermouth is flavoured with blends of herbs and spices. As each producer has their own special blend, the taste (and quality) of vermouth varies between brands. If you would like to add a bit of "heat", add a drop or two of Tabasco sauce.

3 tbsp finely chopped coriander

Finely grated zest and juice of 2 limes

2 tbsp dry white vermouth

2 cloves garlic, crushed

50 ml/¼ cup olive oil

Tabasco sauce (optional)

Freshly ground black pepper

Combine all the ingredients in a small bowl and mix well.

Makes 175 ml/¾ cup

Hot soy sauce

This glaze is precooked and then brushed over the food during the last few minutes of cooking. It goes well with fish, seafood, chicken or pork.

2 tbsp olive oil

2 fresh red chillies, deseeded and chopped finely

2 tsp grated root ginger

2 cloves garlic, crushed

125 ml/½ cup dry white wine

4 tbsp soy sauce

2 tbsp packed dark brown sugar

2 tsp cornflour

1 tbsp lemon juice

1 Heat the oil in a frying pan and add the chilli, ginger and garlic. Cook, stirring frequently, 1 to 2 minutes. Do not brown.

2 In a separate bowl, whisk together the wine, soy sauce, brown sugar and cornflour and add to the frying pan.

3 Bring to the boil, stirring, until thickened. Pour the sauce into a bowl and let cool.

4 Stir the lemon juice into the cooled sauce.

5 Brush the glaze over the food you are cooking during the final 15 minutes of grilling. Cook over medium heat to prevent the glaze from browning too quickly.

Makes 125 ml/½ cup

Above left Teriyaki red wine marinade **right** Hot soy sauce

Sesame lime marinade

The sesame oil in this marinade creates a wonderfully nutty flavour that is balanced by the citric tartness of the lime juice. Use this mixture on chicken, fish and seafood.

2 tbsp sesame oil

2 tbsp rice vinegar

2 tbsp lime juice

2 tbsp light soy sauce

2 tsp sugar

Combine the ingredients in a medium bowl and mix well.

Makes 125 ml/^{1}/$_2$ cup

White wine marinade

This classic wine marinade imparts a delicate action on chicken and fish. The coriander will give it a peppery kick. You could substitute parsley if you prefer a very subtle marinade flavour.

 4 tbsp dry white wine

2 tbsp lemon juice

6 tbsp olive oil

1 garlic clove, crushed

1 small red onion, chopped finely

2 tbsp finely chopped coriander

2 bay leaves, crumbled

Freshly ground black pepper

Combine the ingredients in a medium bowl and mix well.

Makes 225 ml/1 cup

Hoisin marinade

Some people think of hoisin sauce as "Chinese ketchup" because, like ketchup, it's a popular condiment. But that's where the similarities end – hoisin is a mixture of soy beans, garlic, chillies and spices with no tomatoes to be found.

225 ml/1 cup hoisin sauce

3 tbsp rice vinegar

2 tbsp light soy sauce

4 cloves garlic, chopped finely

^{1}/$_4$ tsp five-spice powder

2 tbsp sesame oil

Dash of Tabasco sauce

Combine the ingredients in a small bowl and mix well.

Makes 350 ml/1^1/$_2$ cups

FISH AND SEAFOOD 3

Spice-rubbed tilapia with mango and red onion salsa

Tilapia is a farm-raised fish with a light and slightly sweet flavour. This dish goes very well with couscous and grilled asparagus.

900 g tilapia (filleted)

FOR THE SALSA

1 ripe mango, peeled and diced

1 red pepper, deseeded and diced

1 red onion, diced

3 tbsp finely chopped coriander

1 tsp crushed garlic

75 ml/⅓ cup fresh lime juice

50 ml/¼ cup pineapple juice

1 tbsp deseeded and finely chopped serrano chilli

Sea salt and freshly ground black pepper, to taste

50 ml/¼ cup olive oil

FOR THE SPICE RUB

1 tbsp ground cumin, toasted

1 tbsp ground coriander

1 tbsp sweet Hungarian paprika

1 tbsp sea salt

1 tbsp freshly ground black pepper

1 Mix all the salsa ingredients in a medium bowl and blend well. Cover and set aside.

2 Combine all the rub ingredients in a small bowl and mix well.

3 Brush the tilapia with the olive oil. Rub the spice mixture onto the oil-coated tilapia. Place the tilapia in a fish-grilling basket and grill over medium heat, 3 to 4 minutes per side, or until the fish flakes easily with a fork. Transfer to a platter or individual plates, top with the salsa and serve.

Serves 4

Mackerel with spicy tomato jam

Mackerel is a very oily, medium-firm fish that contains a high level of vitamin A, so this comforting dish is very good for you. Mackerel is at its best around spring and summer.

450 g tomatoes, skinned, deseeded and chopped

1 medium Spanish onion, diced

125 ml/½ cup apple jelly

50 ml/¼ cup cider vinegar

1 tbsp chopped tarragon

1 tsp sea salt

½ to 1 tsp crushed red chilli pepper

Four 225-g mackerel fillets, cleaned, with heads removed but with skin left on

Olive oil

Garlic salt and freshly ground black pepper, to taste

Sprigs tarragon and orange slices, to garnish

1 Combine the tomato, onion, jelly, vinegar, tarragon, salt and red chilli pepper in a medium saucepan. Bring to the boil over a medium-high heat. Reduce the heat to medium-low and cook, stirring frequently, 35 to 45 minutes or until thick. Cool the jam to room temperature.

2 Season the mackerel with salt and pepper and brush the skin with olive oil. Grill, skin side down, covered, over medium-hot heat, 5 minutes on each side. Do not turn the fish or overcook it.

3 To serve, top each fillet with 2 tablespoons of tomato jam and season to taste. Garnish with tarragon and orange slices.

Serves 4

Opposite Mackerel with spicy tomato jam

Swordfish kebabs with bay leaf and lemon marinade

For those of you who like swordfish, this recipe is a real treat. If you serve it at your next party, your guests will ask for the recipe.

FOR THE MARINADE

1 tsp grated lemon zest

50 ml/¼ cup fresh lemon juice

50 ml/¼ cup olive oil

2 cloves garlic, crushed

2 tsp packed light
  brown sugar

1 tsp sea salt

1 tsp freshly ground black
  pepper

8 bay leaves

Four 1-cm thick slices
  lemon, each cut in half

450 g swordfish steaks, cut
  into 4-cm squares
  (approximately 20 pieces)

4 large cherry tomatoes

Half yellow pepper, cut
  into four

4 metal skewers

Olive oil

1 Combine all the marinade ingredients except the swordfish in a resealable plastic bag. Add the swordfish, seal and turn to coat. Leave to marinate in the refrigerator for 1 hour, turning the bag occasionally.

2 Remove the swordfish from the bag and reserve the marinade. Thread five pieces of swordfish onto each skewer, alternating with a bay leaf and lemon slice taken from the marinade, along with a cherry tomato and pepper square. Keep 50 ml/¼ cup of the marinade for basting and discard the rest.

3 Thoroughly brush the kebabs with olive oil and grill over medium-hot heat, basting occasionally. Turn onto each of the four sides, about 3 minutes per side, or until the fish flakes easily with a fork.

Grilled swordfish steaks

I like to serve this swordfish with a fruit salsa, and it also goes very well with rosé wine.

1 tbsp ground cumin, toasted

1 tsp sea salt

½ tsp freshly ground
  black pepper

¼ tsp chipotle chilli powder

2 tbsp olive oil

Four 150 to 225-g swordfish
  steaks

2 tbsp finely chopped
  parsley

1 lime, quartered

1 Combine the cumin, salt, pepper and chilli powder in a small bowl and blend well.

2 Generously sprinkle the seasoning over the steaks, gently pressing the spices into the fish. Be sure to season both sides. Loosely cover the steaks and set aside for 15 to 20 minutes.

3 Pour the olive oil onto a small plate. Dip each steak in the oil and grill over medium-high heat, 4 to 5 minutes per side or until the fish flakes easily with a fork. Transfer to a platter or individual plates and garnish with parsley and a lime wedge.

Serves 4

Opposite Grilled swordfish steaks

Jamaican jerked sea bass with tropical salsa

Spicy, spicy, spicy – that's the best way to describe this fish. You can make it as hot or as mild as you like by adjusting the quantity of hot peppers you use.

FOR THE JERK MARINADE

50 ml/¼ cup white vinegar

Zest of 1 lime

Juice of 2 limes

3 tbsp vegetable oil

2 cloves garlic, chopped

½ to 2 Scotch bonnet chilli peppers, deseeded and chopped finely

1 tbsp sugar

2 tsp grated root ginger

2 tsp allspice

2 tsp ground thyme

1 tsp ground cinnamon

½ tsp sea salt

½ tsp freshly ground black pepper

½ tsp cayenne pepper

FOR THE TROPICAL SALSA

200 g diced pineapple

75 g diced mango

100 g diced red pepper

100 g peeled, deseeded and diced plum tomatoes

50 g diced red onion

50 g diced cucumber

2 tbsp fresh lime juice

2 tbsp chopped fresh mint

1 tbsp chopped coriander

1 tbsp chopped parsley

1 tbsp deseeded and chopped canned chipotle peppers in adobo sauce

Sea salt and freshly ground black pepper

Six 200-g sea bass fillets

1 Combine the marinade ingredients in a blender until smooth. Place the sea bass in a glass dish and add the marinade, making sure the fish is well coated. Cover and marinate in the refrigerator for 30 to 45 minutes.

2 Combine the salsa ingredients in a bowl and toss gently to blend. Cover and refrigerate for at least 1 hour to allow the flavours to develop.

4 Remove the sea bass from the marinade. Grill over medium-hot heat for 4 to 5 minutes per side. Serve, topped with salsa.

Serves 6

Barbecue-glazed red snapper

Red snapper is a very tasty and popular fish. Buy your fish from a fishmonger you can trust to ensure you'll be using the freshest fish for this recipe.

1 small onion, chopped

1 tbsp packed dark brown sugar

50 ml/¼ cup cider vinegar

2 tbsp ketchup

2 tbsp prepared yellow mustard

1 tbsp Worcestershire sauce

1 tsp chilli powder

½ tsp sea salt

½ tsp freshly ground black pepper

¼ tsp ground cloves

¼ tsp cayenne pepper

700 g red snapper fillets

Olive oil

1 Combine all the ingredients except the fish and olive oil in a small saucepan over medium-high heat. Bring to the boil. Reduce the heat and simmer, stirring occasionally, until the sauce is reduced to a syrup-like consistency, about 3 to 4 minutes. Strain and chill the syrup.

2 Place the red snapper in a glass baking dish and thoroughly coat with the syrup by brushing or spooning it over the fillets. Cover and marinate in the refrigerator for 1 hour.

3 Brush both sides of the red snapper lightly with olive oil and grill over medium-hot heat, basting with the remaining syrup, 4 to 5 minutes per side or until the fish flakes easily with a fork.

Serves 4 to 6

Seared tuna with Cuban Mojito sauce

This simple grilled tuna dish is twice-flavoured, first with a spicy marinade, then with homemade Cuban Mojito sauce, an orange-lime-garlic blend that can be used as a marinade for fish or as a sauce after cooking. Grilling is the perfect way to cook tuna, because the outside is seared, leaving the inside pink and juicy.

4 tuna steaks (170 g each)

3 cloves garlic

1 tsp sea salt

½ tsp cumin

Juice of 1 orange

Juice of 1 lime

Freshly ground black pepper

Cayenne pepper, to taste

2 tbsp olive oil, or as needed

FOR THE MOJITO SAUCE

225 ml/1 cup orange juice

Juice of 1 lime

125 ml/½ cup olive oil

3 cloves garlic, crushed

2 tbsp finely chopped bacon

1 tbsp dry sherry

1 tsp salt

1 tsp dried oregano

1 tsp ground cumin

1 tbsp grated root ginger

1 Combine the garlic, salt, cumin, orange and lime juice, black pepper and cayenne pepper in a medium bowl and mix well.

2 Place the tuna in a glass baking dish. Pour the marinade over the tuna, turning to coat all sides. Cover and leave to marinate about 30 minutes.

3 Remove the tuna from the marinade and pat dry.

4 Meanwhile, prepare the mojito sauce. Place all the mojito sauce ingredients in a jar and shake well until thoroughly blended.

5 Grill the tuna over high heat, about 1 to 2 minutes per side. Serve with the mojito sauce.

Serves 4

Spice-crusted tuna with vegetables and tofu

Cooking time for the tuna will depend on how thick the steaks are and how rare you like your fish. Allow between 1 to 2 minutes per side over a fairly brisk heat.

4 tuna steaks

2 tbsp coriander seeds, finely crushed

1 tsp chilli sauce

2 tsp root ginger purée

250 g trimmed green beans

1 bunch asparagus

1 bunch spring onions, trimmed

3 tbsp vegetable oil

2 tbsp unsalted butter

250 g firm tofu, cut into 5-cm long sticks

Juice of 2 limes

Small bunch of coriander

4 tbsp chopped parsley

1 Place the tuna steaks in a glass baking dish. Combine the coriander seeds, chilli sauce and ginger purée in a small bowl and spread over the fish. Cover and marinate in the refrigerator for about 1 hour.

2 Steam the green beans, asparagus and spring onions for 5 minutes until just tender. Keep them warm in a low oven.

3 Melt the oil and butter in a saucepan over low heat. Transfer to a shallow dish and dip the spice-side of the tuna steaks into the mixture. Grill over hot heat, spice-side down, 2 to 3 minutes, turn and then cook an additional 1 to 2 minutes, or to the doneness you desire.

4 Toss the tofu with the remaining butter and oil and grill over medium-high heat until heated through, 2 to 3 minutes. Remove from the heat and squeeze the lime juice over the tofu. To serve, arrange the vegetables and tofu on serving plates with the tuna steaks on top. Tuck a few coriander leaves among the vegetables and tofu, and scatter with parsley.

Serves 4

Chilli cod and avocado salsa

This is a dish with a real Mexican theme, and it is fairly hot and spicy.

4 skinless cod fillets

FOR THE AVOCADO SALSA
1 large, ripe avocado
2 tbsp fresh lemon juice
1 tomato, peeled, deseeded and chopped
1 onion, chopped finely
Freshly ground black pepper, to taste

FOR THE MARINADE
1 tbsp lime juice
1 onion, chopped
1 red pepper, chopped
2 cloves garlic, crushed
2 red chillies, chopped
2 tbsp light soy sauce
150 ml/²/₃ cup fish stock
1 tsp chilli powder

1 To make the avocado salsa, halve and stone the avocado. Peel and place in a blender or food processor with the lemon juice and blend until smooth, about 10 seconds. Transfer to a bowl and add the tomato, onion and pepper. Cover and chill in the refrigerator until needed.

2 Place the cod fillets on four squares of heavy-duty foil. Put the remaining marinade ingredients in a blender and blend for 10 seconds. Spread the marinade on to the cod and close the parcels around the fish, being sure to secure the seams.

3 Grill over medium heat 10 to 15 minutes. Serve with the avocado salsa.

Serves 4

Salmon and tomato packets

Wrap salmon fillets in foil and cook them on the grill, and you'll be well on your way to a dinner with almost nothing to clean. Just crumple up the foil, throw it away and the dishes are done.

2 tbsp unsalted butter
Six 4-cm thick skinless salmon fillets
6 tomatoes, cut into wedges
6 spring onions (white and green parts), chopped
2 tbsp olive oil

1 tbsp fresh lemon juice
1 tsp caster sugar
Whole or chopped herbs, such as dill, coriander and parsley

1 Cut six large squares of heavy-duty foil. Butter the foil and lay a salmon fillet on each square. Top with some tomato wedges and a sprinkling of spring onions.

2 Whisk together the oil, lemon juice and sugar. Drizzle it over the salmon. Add a few sprigs of herbs to the parcels.

3 Close the parcels, being sure to secure the seams. Grill over medium-hot heat, turning occasionally, 8 to 10 minutes. Carefully open the parcels to avoid the steam, and serve immediately.

Serves 6

Opposite Salmon and tomato packets

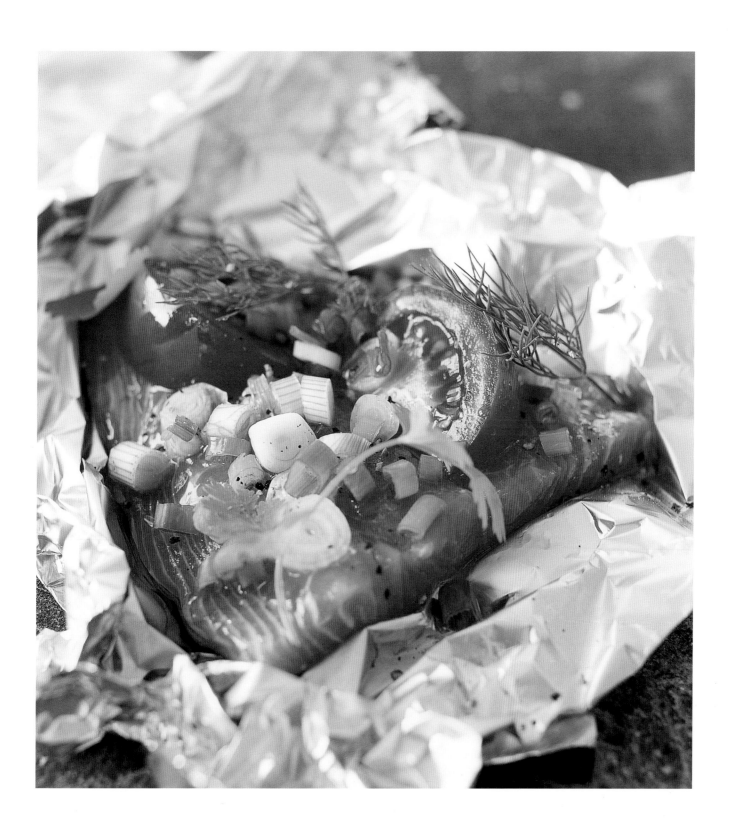

Orange-and-chilli marinated sardines

Sardines cooked this way are simply delicious. Use lime juice instead of orange, if you prefer. Use a grill basket designed for fish if you have one.

8 to 12 fresh sardines, cleaned

125 ml/½ cup fresh orange juice

4 tbsp olive oil

1 to 4 jalapeño chillies,
deseeded and sliced finely

1 tbsp packed light brown sugar

Sprigs of fresh rosemary

Orange wedges

1 Wipe or lightly rinse the sardines and pat dry with kitchen paper. Place in a glass baking dish.

2 Combine the orange juice, oil, chilli and brown sugar in a small bowl. Pour the mixture over the sardines and add some springs of rosemary. Cover and marinate in the refrigerator at least 2 hours, turning occasionally.

3 Grill the sardines over medium heat, basting with the marinade at least once during cooking, 3 to 4 minutes or until cooked through.

4 Garnish with orange wedges and sprigs of rosemary.

Serves 4

Right Orange-and-chilli marinated sardines

Stuffed red mullet

Grape leaves are usually preserved in brine, so it's important to soak them thoroughly before use.

12 to 16 grape leaves, depending upon size

Boiling water

4 small red mullet or other small whole fish, cleaned and scaled

2 tbsp olive oil

4 spring onions (green and white parts), chopped

75 g dried apricots, chopped finely

2 tbsp chopped hazelnuts

1 tbsp grated orange zest

1 tbsp chopped fresh dill

50 g fresh breadcrumbs

Sea salt and freshly ground black pepper, to taste

1 medium egg yolk

2 to 3 tbsp orange juice

Olive oil

1 Cover the grape leaves with boiling water and leave for 20 minutes. Drain and rinse thoroughly with boiling water. Pat dry with kitchen paper and set aside.

2 Heat 2 teaspoons of the oil in a frying pan and sauté the spring onions for 2 minutes. Remove from the heat and add the apricots, hazelnuts, orange zest, dill, breadcrumbs, salt and pepper. Mix in the egg yolk and enough orange juice to give the mixture a stiff consistency.

3 Use the stuffing to fill the cavities of the fish. Wrap each fish in the grape leaves, encasing them completely, and secure with either soaked twine or cocktail sticks.

4 Oil the grill with olive oil and cook the fish over a medium heat, 4 to 6 minutes per side, or until done and the grape leaves are charred.

5 Remove the twine or cocktail sticks and serve.

Serves 4

Grilled halibut steak with Caribbean marinade

Halibut steaks are a great alternative to salmon steaks, especially if you want a less oily fish. They are thick enough to stand up to grilling without the aid of a grill basket, which can't be said for a lot of other white-fleshed fish.

2 tbsp red wine vinegar
1 large onion, grated
2 tbsp tomato purée
4 cloves garlic, crushed
2 tsp packed brown sugar
1 to 2 tbsp red chilli paste (optional)
2 tsp anchovy paste
4 halibut steaks (250 g each)

1 Combine all the ingredients except the halibut in a small bowl and mix well.

2 Place the fish in a glass baking dish. Pour the marinade over the fish, turning to coat all sides. Cover and marinate for 1 hour.

3 Remove the halibut from the dish, reserving some of the marinade. Grill over hot heat for about 6 minutes per side, brushing with the marinade while cooking.

Serves 4

Barbecued halibut steaks

Serve this fish with a fruit salsa, a tartar sauce made with mayonnaise, and hard-boiled eggs, or even hollandaise sauce. It's very versatile and very delicious.

2 tbsp unsalted butter
2 tbsp packed light brown sugar
3 cloves garlic, crushed
2 tbsp fresh lemon juice
2 tbsp soy sauce
½ tsp freshly ground black pepper
¼ tsp cayenne pepper
700 g halibut steaks

1 Combine all the ingredients except the fish in a small saucepan and heat until the butter melts and the sugar dissolves. Cool to room temperature.

2 Coat the halibut with the sauce and grill over medium-hot heat, frequently basting with the sauce, 5 to 7 minutes per side, or until the fish flakes easily with a fork.

Serves 4

Grilled trout with bacon

An unusual combination; however, the salt of the bacon gives the trout a lip-smacking edge.

4 trout, at least 350 g each
Sea salt and freshly ground
  black pepper, to taste
8 bacon rashers
4 bay leaves

1 Season the trout with the salt and pepper. Wrap two rashers of bacon around each trout and tuck a bay leaf inside a fold in the bacon, but be sure the bay leaf is also touching the fish.

2 Brush the rack with oil and grill the trout over hot heat, 4 to 6 minutes per side. Serve immediately.

Serves 4

Opposite Grilled halibut steak with Caribbean marinade

Crab cakes with honey mustard sauce

As an accompaniment to these special crab cakes, I suggest serving foil-wrapped squash and apples with brown sugar (see page 124), alongside a tossed salad or coleslaw.

**FOR THE HONEY
MUSTARD SAUCE**

50 ml/¼ cup light honey

50 ml/¼ cup Dijon mustard

1 shallot, minced

2 tsp sugar

¼ tsp curry powder

¾ tsp celery deseed

2 tbsp rice vinegar

2 to 3 drops Tabasco sauce

FOR THE CRAB CAKES

450 g fresh or canned
   crabmeat, picked
   clean of shell

75 ml/⅓ cup mayonnaise

2 tsp dried mustard

1 tsp Worcestershire sauce

¼ tsp seasoned salt

¼ tsp white pepper

25 g diced pimento

25 g diced green pepper

75 g finely chopped onion

30 to 40 g fresh,
   unseasoned breadcrumbs

Olive oil

1 Combine all the honey mustard sauce ingredients in a small bowl and blend well. Set aside.

2 Flake the crabmeat with a fork. In a large bowl, whisk together the mayonnaise, mustard, Worcestershire sauce, salt and pepper. Add the crabmeat, pimento, green pepper and onion. Fold in the breadcrumbs and blend well. Add more breadcrumbs if needed to hold the mixture together. Form into 6 to 8 cakes.

3 Place the crab cakes on a baking sheet and refrigerate for 2 to 3 hours or until firm. Brush both sides of the cakes with olive oil and grill over medium-hot heat, 4 to 5 minutes per side or until done. Use a grill basket if you have one, as it makes turning much easier. Serve with the honey mustard sauce.

Serves 4

Crab quesadillas with mango salsa

This dish is excellent as a starter before dinner, or served as an appetiser for your next get-together with friends.

FOR THE MANGO SALSA

1 ripe mango, peeled
   and diced

2 plum tomatoes, deseeded
   and diced

3 spring onions, thinly sliced
   (green and white parts)

Juice of 1 lime

2 tbsp chopped fresh mint

2 tbsp raspberry vinegar

½ tsp sea salt

¼ tsp freshly ground
   black pepper

FOR THE QUESADILLAS

350 g shredded cooked
   crabmeat

150 g Monterey Jack or
   Cheddar cheese, grated

1 avocado, diced

100 g chopped spring onions
   (white and green parts)

3 tbsp chopped coriander

25 g chopped, roasted red
   pepper

2 tbsp fresh lime juice

Sea salt and freshly ground
   black pepper

2 tbsp olive oil

Six 20-cm flour tortillas

1 Combine all the salsa ingredients in a medium bowl and gently toss. Cover and chill at least 1 hour so the flavours can develop.

2 For the quesadillas, combine all the ingredients except the oil and tortillas in a medium bowl and gently toss, being sure to mix the ingredients thoroughly.

3 Brush one side of two tortillas with olive oil. Place one tortilla, oil side down, on a grill that is medium hot. Spread with the crabmeat mixture and then top with the second tortilla, oil side up, pressing down on the tortilla with a spatula. Place on the grill, cover and cook about 4 to 5 minutes. Turn the quesadilla and cook, covered, for another 3 to 4 minutes or until the cheese has melted. Transfer to a board and cut in half, then cut each half into pie-shaped pieces. Serve with the mango salsa.

Serves 4

Above left Crab cakes with honey mustard sauce **right** Crab quesadillas with mango salsa

Grilled oysters Palatine

These oysters are one of my party favourites – they're so easy to make. You and your guests can stand around the grill while they cook. Just make sure you have a good lager in your hands.

FOR THE FILLING

2 tbsp unsalted butter

450 g chopped frozen spinach, thawed

1 tsp sea salt

½ tsp white pepper

¼ tsp ground mace

FOR THE SAUCE

150 g unsalted butter

5 large egg yolks

2 tbsp fresh lemon juice

2 tbsp dry vermouth

2 dashes Tabasco sauce, or to taste

Sea salt, to taste

1 tsp curry powder, or to taste

24 oysters on the half shell, drained of most of their liquor

1 For the filling, place the butter and spinach in a pan over medium heat and cook, stirring occasionally, until the spinach is tender, about 15 minutes. Strain in a colander and squeeze out excess liquid with the back of a spoon. Season with pepper, mace and salt and set aside to cool completely.

2 For the sauce, melt the butter in a small pan over medium heat until foamy. Do not let it brown. Put the egg yolks, lemon juice, vermouth, Tabasco sauce and salt in a blender. Blend for 5 seconds at medium speed. Increase to high speed and slowly pour in half the melted butter while the blender is running, for about 30 seconds. Sprinkle the curry powder over the emulsion. Blend again at high and slowly add the remaining butter while the blender is running, about 15 seconds. Taste the sauce and adjust the curry powder if necessary.

3 Divide the spinach mixture among the 24 shells, place an oyster on top and add a dollop of hollandaise sauce. Grill the oysters over hot heat for about 5 minutes or until they are bubbly and cooked.

Serves 4 to 6

Grilled Cheddar oysters

As long as there are oysters around, I'll be there to grill them. These are delicious and slightly unusual. They make a great treat accompanied by a crisp white wine.

FOR THE FILLING

1 tsp arrowroot

1 tbsp cold water

2 tbsp butter

1 leek, cleaned and sliced

2 cloves garlic, crushed

1 cob fresh corn, husked, grilled and kernels cut off the cob

225 ml double cream

Pinch of mace

50 g grated strong Cheddar cheese

1 leek, sliced finely, to garnish

Sea salt and freshly ground black pepper, to taste

FOR THE TOPPING

2 rashers smoked bacon, cooked crisp and crumbled

75 g plain breadcrumbs

2 tbsp olive oil

24 oysters on the half shell

1 Mix the arrowroot and cold water and set aside.

2 Melt the butter in a saucepan and sauté the leek, garlic and corn over a medium heat until the leek is soft and tender. Add the cream and mace and bring to the boil. Reduce the heat and simmer. Thicken slightly by adding the arrowroot and water mixture, stirring the mixture again before adding it to the pan. Remove from the heat and blend in the cheese with a wire whisk. Season with salt and pepper.

3 Combine the topping ingredients except for the oysters in a medium bowl and blend well.

4 To assemble, top each oyster in its shell with some of the filling and sprinkle with some of the topping. Grill over a medium heat for 5 minutes, covered, until the oysters are hot and bubbly. Serve garnished with shredded leek and crushed sea salt, if desired.

Serves 4 to 6

Opposite Grilled oysters Palatine

Asian prawns with honey-tea dipping sauce

I like serving this Asian delight on a bed of citrus rice fried in a little ginger and garlic. To make extra-strong tea, simply use two tea bags with the usual amount of boiling water for one cup.

Cup of extra-strong orange spiced tea, cooled

125 ml/½ cup honey

125 ml/½ cup sweet rice vinegar

1 tbsp fresh lemon juice

1 tbsp grated root ginger

1 clove garlic, crushed

1 tsp ground coriander

½ tsp ground black pepper

700 g medium prawns (shrimp), peeled and deveined, with tails left on

Garlic salt, to taste

4 spring onions, thinly sliced (white and green parts)

Orange wedges

8 metal skewers

1 Combine the tea, honey, vinegar, lemon juice, ginger, garlic, coriander and pepper and blend well. Reserve 125 ml/½ cup of the marinade, cover and set aside.

2 Place the prawns and the marinade in a resealable plastic bag, seal and turn to coat. Marinate in the refrigerator for at least 30 to 45 minutes.

3 Remove the prawns from the bag, discarding the marinade. Thread them onto eight skewers, dividing them evenly, and alternating with orange wedges. Grill over medium heat, turning only once, for 4 to 6 minutes or until the prawns (shrimp) are just pink and firm to the touch. Be careful not to overcook. Season with garlic salt to taste.

4 To prepare the dipping sauce, add the reserved marinade to a pan. Bring to the boil over medium heat and reduce the sauce slightly, about 3 to 5 minutes. Stir in the spring onion. Serve hot.

Serves 4 to 6

Opposite Asian prawns with honey-tea dipping sauce

Creamy lobster sauce with fettuccine

To prepare lobster for this delectable pasta dish, it is first removed from the shell, then grilled and coated in garlic butter. Your mouth will water as you read the recipe.

125 ml/½ cup white wine

2 tbsp sherry wine vinegar

125 ml/½ cup fish stock

50 g finely chopped shallots

450 ml/2 cups double cream

2 ripe avocados, diced

8 plum tomatoes, peeled and diced

100 g unsalted butter, softened

2 cloves garlic, crushed

450 g fettucine pasta

Sea salt and freshly ground black pepper, to taste

One 450- to 550-g lobster tail

Chopped fresh parsley, to garnish

1 Combine the wine, vinegar, fish stock and shallots in a medium pan over medium heat. Bring to the boil stirring continually until the liquid has reduced its volume to 125 ml/½ cup. Add the cream, avocado and tomatoes and bring back to the boil. Reduce the heat and simmer until reduced and thickened, about 2 to 3 minutes. Season with salt and pepper.

2 Combine the butter and garlic in a small pan and melt over medium-low heat. Set aside.

3 Cook the pasta in a large pot of boiling, salted water until tender but still firm (al dente). Drain, set aside and keep warm.

4 Split the lobster tail, devein it and remove the meat from the shell. Thoroughly brush the lobster meat on all sides with the garlic butter. Grill over medium-hot heat, 4 to 5 minutes per side, or until the meat is opaque and white. Remove from the grill, chop the meat and add it to the cream sauce. Blend well.

5 Transfer the warm pasta to a serving platter and top with the lobster sauce. Garnish with the parsley and serve.

Serves 4 to 6

Above left Scallops with courgettes and tomato pasta **right** Scallop and prawn brochettes

Scallops with courgettes and tomato pasta

Grilled scallops are sweet, tasty and easy to cook. Here is a great meal that can be made in about 30 minutes or less.

450 g linguini pasta

50 ml/¼ cup olive oil

4 cloves garlic, crushed

2 medium courgettes (zucchini), diced

1 tsp sea salt

1 tsp freshly ground black pepper

½ tsp crushed red pepper

50 g chopped basil leaves

4 plum tomatoes, diced

700 g sea scallops

Olive oil

2 tbsp freshly grated Parmesan

1 Cook the pasta in a large pot of boiling, salted water until tender but still firm (al dente).

2 In a frying pan on the hob or on your grill, heat the oil and sauté the garlic for 1 minute. Add the courgettes, salt, pepper and red pepper and sauté over a medium heat for 8 to 10 minutes or until tender and crisp. Add the basil and tomato and simmer for 5 to 7 minutes. Remove from the heat and keep warm.

3 Brush the scallops with olive oil and grill over medium-hot heat, 3 minutes per side, until the scallops are opaque. Remove the scallops, quarter them and add to the sauce mixture.

4 Transfer the pasta to a large serving platter or bowl. Pour the sauce over the cooked pasta and sprinkle with the Parmesan.

Serves 4 to 6

Scallop and prawn brochettes

Scallops and prawns are a no-fail shellfish combination. This herb-infused marinade adds just enough flavour to these tasty beauties. Keep a careful eye on the brochettes because the scallops and prawns don't take long to cook.

FOR THE MARINADE

225 ml/1 cup dry white wine

2 tbsp balsamic vinegar

2 tbsp fresh lemon juice

50 ml/¼ cup vegetable oil

1 tbsp finely chopped tarragon

1 tsp finely chopped basil

1 tsp finely chopped thyme

1 tsp finely chopped oregano

1 tsp sugar

Sea salt and freshly ground black pepper

450 to 900 g scallops, shucked and rinsed

450 to 900 g prawns, peeled and deveined

225 g unsalted butter, melted

2 tbsp fresh lemon juice

2 tsp freshly ground black pepper

1 tsp paprika

1 lemon, cut into wedges

6 metal skewers

1 Combine the wine, vinegar, lemon juice, oil, herbs, sugar, salt and pepper in a glass bowl and mix well with a wire whisk. Place the scallops and prawns in the marinade, tossing to coat evenly. Cover and marinate in the refrigerator for 30 minutes to 1 hour.

2 Drain the scallops and prawns and thread them on to long metal skewers, threading the scallops through their diameter. Combine the melted butter and lemon juice. Brush the scallops and prawns with the butter mixture and season with pepper and paprika.

3 Grill over hot heat, basting with the butter-lemon mixture every 3 to 4 minutes, 6 to 8 minutes per side, or until done, being careful not to overcook.

Serves 6 to 8

Grilled octopus and peppers

The first time I had the pleasure of eating octopus, I was in Hawaii. It took a little work to make, but the results were worth the effort. Once you try this dish, I think you'll agree.

Small octopus (about 450 g)

125 ml/½ cup fresh lemon juice

50 ml/¼ cup olive oil

4 cloves garlic, crushed

½ tsp dried oregano

½ tsp dried marjoram

1 tsp sea salt

**½ tsp freshly ground
    black pepper**

2 tbsp olive oil

1 green pepper

1 red pepper

1 yellow pepper

FOR THE DRESSING

125 ml/½ cup olive oil

2 tbsp balsamic vinegar

1 tbsp fresh lemon juice

1 tbsp sugar

2 cloves garlic, crushed

1 tbsp finely chopped parsley

½ tsp sea salt

**½ tsp freshly ground
    black pepper**

Lemon wedges, to serve

1 Cut the octopus into strips or leave whole if small. Rinse well and place in a glass bowl. Add the lemon juice, oil, garlic, oregano, marjoram, salt and pepper. Cover and marinate in the refrigerator for 24 hours, stirring occasionally.

2 Brush the skin of the peppers with 2 tablespoons of olive oil. Grill over hot heat until the skin blisters all over, approximately 4 to 5 minutes. Remove from the heat and place in a sealed paper bag. Leave to rest about 20 minutes.

3 For the dressing, combine all the ingredients in a small bowl and blend well.

4 Remove the peppers from the bag and, using a towel, rub off the skins. Deseed and remove the membranes. Slice the peppers into strips and arrange on a serving plate, alternating the colours. Drizzle with half the dressing and set aside.

5 Remove the octopus from the bowl and reserve the marinade. Grill the octopus over hot heat, turning frequently and basting with the reserved marinade, 15 to 20 minutes. Remove from the grill, cut into bite-sized pieces and pile in the middle of the plate of peppers. Drizzle with the remaining dressing and serve, accompanied with lemon wedges to squeeze over.

Serves 2 to 4

Paella

A one-dish meal, paella provides a wonderful variety of tastes and textures. Let people help themselves straight from the pan. If you have a small grill, cook the rice in advance, add the oil and lemon dressing and let it cool to room temperature. Then, cook all the extras on the grill and pile them high, hot, on to the cooled rice.

6 tbsp olive oil, plus extra for brushing

3 tbsp fresh lemon juice

2 tbsp honey

8 chicken thighs

16 large prawns (shrimp)

350 g mussels

175 ml/³/₄ cup dry white wine, plus 3 tbsp for the mussels

50 g unsalted butter

1 onion, chopped finely

2 red peppers, deseeded and sliced

2 cloves garlic, crushed

450 g risotto rice, such as Arborio

About 1 l/4¹/₂ cups hot vegetable or chicken stock

4 tomatoes, peeled and chopped

¹/₂ tsp ground saffron

Sea salt and freshly ground pepper, to taste

3 tbsp chopped parsley

Lemon wedges

1 Whisk together 3 tablespoons of the oil with the lemon juice and honey and set aside. Brush the chicken thighs and the prawns (shrimp) with this dressing. Pile the mussels onto a large piece of heavy-duty foil and add 3 tablespoons of the wine and the butter. Wrap loosely (you may need to allow space for the mussels to expand as they open), close the parcel and gather the seams towards the top.

2 Heat the remaining oil in a large paella dish or large shallow frying pan and add the onion, pepper and garlic. Cook gently, stirring frequently, until the vegetables are soft but not brown, about 10 minutes.

3 Add the rice and cook 1 to 2 minutes, stirring.

4 Pour in about one quarter of the hot stock and the 175 ml/³/₄ cup wine. Add the tomato, saffron, salt and pepper. Heat, stirring occasionally, until the mixture comes to the boil. Then simmer gently, adding extra hot stock each time the rice has absorbed most of the liquid, until the rice is plump and tender. Do not allow the rice to dry out completely – it should stay quite moist.

5 Meanwhile, grill the chicken thighs over medium-hot heat, turning occasionally, for 15 to 20 minutes.

6 Ten minutes after placing the chicken thighs on the grill, start to grill the parcel of mussels, seam side up, along with the prawns (shrimp). Cook, turning the prawns (shrimp) occasionally (but not the foil parcel), until you can hear the mussels sizzling and the parcel feels full, and the prawns (shrimp) are pink and cooked, about 10 minutes.

7 Add the oil and lemon dressing to the rice. Tear open the foil parcel and pour the mussels and their butter juices into the rice, discarding any mussels that have not opened. Add the chicken, prawns (shrimp) and parsley and stir gently. Serve immediately with lemon wedges.

Serves 8

POULTRY AND GAME 4

Blueberry grilled chicken

Blueberries are not usually associated with grilled chicken, or grilled anything for that matter, but don't let that fool you. When you taste this chicken, you'll wonder why you haven't tried this combination sooner.

Four 100 to 125-g boneless, skinless chicken breasts

125 ml/½ cup apricot jam

125 ml/½ cup raspberry vinegar

4 tbsp spicy brown mustard

1 tsp sea salt

½ tsp freshly ground black pepper

¼ tsp cayenne pepper

25 g blueberries

1 Place the jam, vinegar, mustard, salt and black pepper in a bowl and mix until well blended. Reserve 150 ml/^{2}/$_3$ cup and set aside.

2 Using a sharp knife, slash criss-cross slices into the chicken flesh. Place the chicken in a glass baking dish. Pour the remaining marinade over the chicken, turning to make sure both sides are coated. Cover and leave to marinate in the refrigerator for 3 to 4 hours. Reserve the remaining marinade.

3 Grill the chicken over medium-hot heat, basting with the reserved marinade, 5 to 7 minutes per side or until the chicken is no longer pink in the middle.

4 Combine the blueberries with the 150 ml/^{2}/$_3$ cup reserved marinade in a saucepan, bring to the boil and serve over the grilled chicken.

Serves 4

Spicy grilled chicken

This is a simple yet delicious way to make chicken. If you're new to grilling, this recipe is a good place to start because chicken legs are very forgiving and easy to cook.

125 ml/½ cup vegetable oil

2 tbsp fresh lime juice

2 tbsp fresh lemon juice

2 tbsp balsamic vinegar

2 cloves garlic, crushed

1 tbsp lemon pepper

1 tsp sea salt

1 tsp lime zest

4 chicken quarters (leg and thigh)

1 Combine all the ingredients except the chicken in a small bowl and blend well. Put the chicken and the marinade in a resealable plastic bag, seal, and turn to coat. Marinate in the refrigerator for 4 hours.

2 Grill the chicken over medium heat, covered, turning as needed, for 35 to 45 minutes or until the juices run clear.

Serves 4 to 8

Opposite Blueberry grilled chicken

Above left Tex-Mex wings **right** Caribbean chicken with warm fruit salsa

Tex-Mex wings

This is an economical dish to prepare for a party, as chicken wings are inexpensive. So be ready to make double, or even more quantities, and have plenty of napkins on hand. Enjoy! To make it easier to turn the wings while grilling, try threading them on to long, flat metal skewers. Alternatively, you can also use a grill basket.

Finely grated zest and juice of 2 oranges

1 tbsp malt vinegar

3 tbsp dark treacle

1 tbsp ground coriander

1 tbsp Tabasco, or to taste

24 chicken wings, bony tips removed

4 to 6 wooden skewers, soaked

1 Put the orange juice and zest into a large nonreactive bowl. Whisk in the vinegar, treacle, coriander and Tabasco sauce. Add the chicken wings and toss until well coated.

2 Cover and marinate in the refrigerator for about 2 hours, stirring occasionally.

3 Remove the wings from the marinade, thread onto the wooden skewers and grill over medium-high heat, turning occasionally and basting with the remaining marinade, 20 to 25 minutes or until crisp and cooked through.

Serves 6

Caribbean chicken with warm fruit salsa

Salsas are very popular and can be made using many different ingredients. The chilli here gives a pleasant, fiery tang. Use as much of the chilli as your palate can take.

FOR THE MARINADE

4 skinless chicken breasts

2 cloves garlic, crushed

½ to 1 habanero chilli, deseeded and finely chopped

1 tbsp grated lime zest

2 tbsp grated root ginger

3 tbsp fresh lime juice

125 ml/½ cup mango or orange juice

2 tbsp chopped coriander

1 tbsp olive oil

Chopped fresh coriander and lime wedges

FOR THE SALSA

1 firm but ripe papaya, peeled and deseeded

1 small fresh pineapple peeled and sliced, or 2 to 3 slices fresh pineapple

2 firm tomatoes, deseeded and chopped

4 spring onions (white and green parts), trimmed and finely chopped

2 tbsp chopped coriander

1 Make three slashes diagonally across each chicken breast and place in a glass baking dish.

2 For the marinade, combine the garlic, chilli, lime zest and ginger in a small bowl. Stir in the fruit juices and coriander. Pour over the chicken and coat all sides. Cover and marinate in the refrigerator for 30 minutes, stirring occasionally.

3 For the salsa, slice the papaya thickly. Brush the fruit and rack with olive oil. Grill over a medium heat until seared on each side. Remove, chop finely and mix with the remaining salsa ingredients.

4 Drain the chicken from the marinade. Grill over medium heat, 5 to 6 minutes per side. Serve garnished with coriander and lime wedges atop 1 to 2 spoonfuls of warm salsa.

Serves 4

Citrus-glazed chicken with pear-gorgonzola salsa

The citrus zing in this glaze brings out the sweetness of the salsa, making for a delightful contrast of flavours in every bite.

FOR THE CITRUS GLAZE

1 tbsp unsalted butter

75 g diced red onion

50 ml/¼ cup orange juice
  concentrate

125 ml/½ cup chicken stock

2 tbsp dark rum

2 tbsp honey

2 tbsp fresh lemon juice

1 tbsp fresh thyme, crushed

1 tsp lemon zest

1 tsp sea salt

**Four 100 to 125-g skinless
  chicken breasts**

FOR THE SALSA

3 medium firm-ripe pears,
  cored and diced

75 g watercress leaves

75 g thinly sliced spring
  onions (white and green
  parts)

40 g crumbled
  gorgonzola cheese

2 tbsp olive oil

2 tbsp white wine vinegar

1 Melt the butter in a frying pan over medium-high heat. Add the onion and sauté until it just begins to soften, 2 to 3 minutes. Add the remaining ingredients except the chicken. Bring to the boil. Reduce the heat and simmer until the mixture is reduced by half. Strain the mixture and set aside.

2 Combine all the salsa ingredients in a medium bowl and gently toss to blend. Cover and set aside, at room temperature.

3 Brush the chicken breasts with the sauce and grill over medium-high heat, brushing frequently and turning once, until golden brown and cooked through, 4 to 5 minutes per side. Transfer to a serving platter and keep warm.

4 Place the remaining sauce in a small pan. Bring to the boil and reduce again to make a glaze, about 2 to 3 minutes. Spoon over the chicken and serve with the salsa.

Serves 4

Opposite Citrus-glazed chicken with pear-gorgonzola sauce

Grilled hot wings

These wings, although great as party food, can be a bit messy. Be sure to have plenty of napkins available for your guests. Try serving them with ranch or blue cheese dressing on the side. Yum!

FOR THE RUB

1 tbsp paprika

1 tsp seasoned salt

1 tsp garlic salt

1 tsp cayenne pepper

½ tsp lemon pepper

½ tsp white pepper

½ tsp ground cumin

24 large chicken wings, tips
  removed

FOR THE WING SAUCE

225 ml/1 cup hot red pepper
  sauce

100 g unsalted butter

2 tbsp fresh lemon juice

1 tbsp Worcestershire sauce

1 tsp garlic salt

1 tsp cayenne pepper

1 Combine all the rub ingredients in a small bowl and blend well.

2 Spread the wings out on a baking sheet and thoroughly dust them all over with the rub.

3 Grill over medium heat, covered, turning as needed about every 7 minutes, for about 15 to 20 minutes. As they are done, remove from the grill and place in a large bowl.

4 Meanwhile, combine the wing sauce ingredients in a saucepan and heat until the butter has melted, but do not let it burn. Set aside and keep warm. Pour the sauce over the cooked wings and toss well to coat. Serve hot.

Serves 4 to 6

Chicken drumsticks with yoghurt marinade

Although you might be tempted to omit one or two of the spices, don't do it. The flavour combination is essential for the success of the dish.

Generous 125 ml/½ cup plain yoghurt

3 cloves garlic, crushed

2.5-cm piece root ginger, peeled and grated

Juice of 1 lemon

1 tsp ground turmeric

1 tsp ground coriander

1 tsp ground cumin

1 tsp garam masala

½ tsp chilli powder

Sea salt, to taste

8 chicken drumsticks

1 Place the chicken drumsticks in a glass baking dish.

2 Combine all the marinade ingredients in a bowl and mix well. Reserve some of the marinade and add the remainder to the chicken, turning to be sure all the pieces are coated. Cover and marinate in the refrigerator overnight, turning occasionally.

3 Grill the chicken drumsticks over medium-hot heat, turning and basting frequently with the reserved marinade, 20 minutes or until the juices run clear when the thickest part of the leg is pierced.

Serves 2 to 4

Chicken and tarragon burgers

These burgers make a sophisticated alternative to beef burgers and are ideal for an informal lunch or dinner party. Serve them with assorted relishes and French fries.

550 g fresh minced chicken

6 spring onions, trimmed and chopped finely

25 g toasted pine kernels

2 tbsp chopped tarragon

1 tbsp paprika

1 tbsp grated lemon zest

Sea salt and freshly ground black pepper, to taste

8 slices prosciutto

Olive oil

4 pitta breads, burger buns or ciabatta rolls

Rocket leaves

1 red onion, peeled and sliced thinly

1 Place the chicken, spring onions, pine kernels, tarragon, paprika, lemon zest and pepper into a food processor and process for 1 minute or until the mixture forms a ball. Remove from the processor bowl and, with dampened hands, shape into four burgers. Lightly cover the burgers and chill in the refrigerator for 30 minutes.

2 Remove from the refrigerator and wrap each burger with 2 slices of prosciutto.

3 Lightly brush the burgers with olive oil and grill over medium heat, 5 to 6 minutes per side or until done.

4 Meanwhile, split the breads, buns or rolls in half and grill, cut-side down, 1 to 2 minutes or until heated.

5 To serve, place inside the warmed bread along with some rocket and sliced onion.

Serves 4

Opposite Chicken and tarragon burgers

Grilled chicken with raspberry-balsamic glaze

Chicken halves are whole chickens that have been cut into two pieces of approximately equal weight. They're great when you want the flavour of a whole chicken, but might not have the time to cook a whole bird.

FOR THE RUB
3 tbsp onion salt
1 tsp freshly ground black pepper
1 tsp dried basil
½ tsp dried thyme
¼ tsp ground celery seed
2 half chickens (1.5 to 1.7 kg)

FOR THE GLAZE
225 ml/1 cup seedless raspberry jam
50 ml/¼ cup balsamic vinegar
1 tbsp orange-flavoured liqueur, such as Triple Sec or Curaçao
1 tsp sea salt
½ tsp freshly ground black pepper

1 Combine the rub ingredients in a small bowl and blend well. Set aside.

2 Rinse the chicken and pat dry with kitchen papers. Thoroughly season the chicken with the rub and set aside.

3 Combine the glaze ingredients in a saucepan and cook over medium heat, stirring with a wire whisk until blended, about 10 minutes.

4 Grill the chicken over medium heat, skin side down, covered, turning every 10 to 15 minutes, for about 1 hour. Brush with the glaze and cook for 5 to 7 minutes more, repeating the glazing at least one more time, or as desired.

Serves 2 to 4

Sweet-and-sour chicken wings

The chicken wings are threaded onto kebab sticks for easy turning on the barbecue. Alternatively, cook them in a grill basket. Serve with grilled yellow peppers.

1 medium onion, chopped
2 cloves garlic
1 small green pepper, deseeded and chopped
4 canned pineapple rings, drained
3 tbsp wine vinegar
2 tbsp soy sauce
1½ tbsp corn oil
1 tbsp sugar
24 chicken wings
Grated lemon zest
8 metal skewers

1 Put all the ingredients except the chicken and the lemon zest into a blender and process until smooth. Pour the mixture into a large, shallow dish. Add the chicken wings and turn until they are well coated. Cover and leave to stand for up to 2 hours at room temperature, or refrigerate for up to 12 hours, turning occasionally.

2 Remove the chicken wings from the marinade and thread them onto 8 skewers. Grill over medium-hot heat, occasionally brushing with the remaining marinade and turning often, until crisp and cooked through, about 20 minutes. To serve, garnish with grated lemon zest.

Serves 6

Opposite Grilled chicken with raspberry-balsamic glaze

Sugar-spiced chicken with gingered mango

To make your chicken the authentic Cuban way, substitute blood orange or sour orange juice for the orange and lime juice. Made either way, this sweet and hot chicken tastes fantastic.

4 split chicken breasts, skinned and flattened to a uniform thickness

FOR THE MARINADE
125 ml/½ cup freshly squeezed orange juice

1 tbsp hot red pepper sauce

Juice of 2 limes

½ tsp sea salt

⅓ tsp freshly ground black pepper

FOR THE RUB
75 g packed light brown sugar

1 tsp dried mustard

1 tsp allspice

1 tsp dried thyme

½ tsp ground cumin

½ tsp cayenne pepper

¼ tsp sea salt

¼ tsp freshly ground black pepper

FOR THE GINGERED MANGO
150 g diced ripe mango

75 g diced red onion

1 to 2 tsp grated root ginger

1 tsp sea salt

1 Combine the marinade ingredients and blend well. Place the chicken breasts and the marinade in a resealable plastic bag, seal and turn to coat. Marinate in the refrigerator for 4 to 6 hours, or overnight.

2 Combine the rub ingredients in a bowl and blend. Remove the chicken from the marinade and dry a little with kitchen paper. Thoroughly season the chicken breasts on all sides with the rub.

3 Combine all the salsa ingredients and gently toss to combine. Cover and refrigerate until required.

4 Grill the chicken breasts over medium-hot heat, turning once, 5 to 7 minutes per side or until the juices run clear. Transfer to serving plates and serve with the gingered mango. Garnish with a lime wedge if desired.

Serves 4

Mediterranean-style poussins

This dish needs to be cooked on a covered barbecue, to ensure that the whole poussins are cooked through yet remain gloriously moist and succulent.

50 g unsalted butter, softened

2 slices prosciutto, chopped finely

2 tbsp finely chopped rosemary

2 sun-dried tomatoes in oil, drained and chopped finely

2 tsp Dijon mustard

Sea salt and freshly ground black pepper, to taste

2 poussins, each weighing about 550 to 700 g

1 small lemon

1 Put the butter, prosciutto, rosemary, tomato and mustard into a small bowl and mix well.

2 Season the poussins lightly with salt and pepper.

3 Carefully lift the skin from the breast of each, running one or two fingers underneath to make a pocket. Spoon half the butter mixture into each pocket and smooth the skin to make a level surface.

4 Wrap each bird in oiled, heavy-duty foil, securing the seams. Grill over medium heat about 30 minutes, turning occasionally.

5 Turn the birds breast side up and, wearing oven mitts, tear open the top of each foil parcel, completely exposing the birds but holding the juices in the foil. Cover the barbecue with the lid and continue cooking another 15 minutes or until the poussins are golden brown and cooked through.

Serves 4

Opposite Mediterranean-style poussins

Lemon-herb poussins

If you can track down divine little poussins, these very young, small chickens are worth the hunt. Their meat is juicy, sweet and delicious.

2 tsp fresh lemon juice	6 poussins
½ tsp sea salt	Sea salt and freshly ground black pepper
75 g unsalted butter	
1 tbsp grated lemon zest	6 sprigs thyme
1 tsp finely chopped thyme	2 lemons, cut into wedges
1 tsp finely chopped rosemary	2 tbsp melted butter
1 clove garlic, crushed	Sprigs of thyme and rosemary, to garnish
¼ tsp freshly ground black pepper	

1 Combine the lemon juice and salt, stirring to dissolve the salt, add the rest of the ingredients down to the poussins and combine until blended well.

2 Rinse the poussins in cold water and pat dry with kitchen paper. Season each cavity with salt and pepper. Working from the cavity end of each bird, run your fingers between the skin and the flesh of the breasts and legs to loosen the skin, being careful not to tear it. Push the lemon-herb butter under the skin and massage the skin from the outside to spread the butter evenly over the breasts and legs.

3 Insert a thyme sprig and lemon wedges into the cavity of each poussin and then tie the legs together with twine. Brush the poussins with melted butter and season with salt and pepper.

4 Grill over medium heat, breast side down and covered, turning every 10 to 15 minutes, for 45 to 55 minutes. Transfer the poussins to a serving platter or plates, remove the string and serve abundantly garnished with thyme and rosemary.

Serves 6

Grilled pheasant

If you have the chance to go pheasant hunting, be sure you know how to properly dress the meat. Pheasant skin is extremely tough and should be removed, feathers and all. If you prefer to buy your pheasant rather than catch it, you'll find it at specialist butchers' shops. Serve the pheasant with a sweet, fruit-based barbecue sauce.

225 ml/1 cup strong cider	2 tbsp finely chopped parsley
125 ml/½ cup vegetable oil	
50 ml/¼ cup soy sauce	2 cloves garlic, crushed
75 g packed dark brown sugar	1 bay leaf
	3 peppercorns
50 ml/¼ cup fresh lemon juice	6 bone-in pheasant breast halves, skin removed
2 tbsp Worcestershire sauce	
2 tbsp grated carrots	Olive oil

1 Combine all the ingredients except the pheasant in a saucepan and bring to the boil over a medium heat. Reduce heat and simmer 5 minutes. Remove from the heat and leave to cool to room temperature.

2 Place the pheasant in a glass baking dish. Pour the remaining marinade over the chicken, turning to make sure both sides are coated. Cover and marinate in the refrigerator for 6 to 8 hours, or overnight.

3 Remove the pheasant from the dish, reserving the remaining marinade, and pat dry with kitchen paper. Thoroughly brush both sides of the pheasant with olive oil and grill over medium heat, turning once and basting with the reserved marinade every 5 minutes, for 15 to 20 minutes or until the juices run clear.

Serves 6

Opposite Lemon-herb poussins

Quail halves with tequila

You might not associate quails with tequila, but this recipe will change your mind. I like serving them with fried potatoes, grilled green beans and a salad or slaw.

1 tbsp garlic salt

2 tsp lemon pepper

1 tsp onion salt

1 tsp sugar

½ tsp celery salt

12 quail halves, breast bones removed

50 ml/¼ cup good-quality gold tequila

50 ml/¼ cup olive oil

1 Combine the garlic salt, lemon pepper, onion salt, sugar and celery salt in a small bowl and blend well. Set aside.

2 Place the quail and the tequila in a resealable plastic bag, seal and turn to coat. Marinate in the refrigerator for 1 hour.

3 Remove the quail from the tequila and pat dry with kitchen paper. Rub with the olive oil and thoroughly season with the spice mixture. Grill the quail over hot heat 3 to 5 minutes per side, being careful not to overcook.

Serves 4 to 6

Opposite Quail halves with tequila

Quail wrapped in grape leaves

Quail are so small that they are more of a starter than a main dish, so you need to cook two, or even three quail per person. This is a traditional method for cooking quail, which infuses the bird with the richness of the bacon and the smoky flavour of the grape leaves.

8 quails

Freshly ground black pepper, to taste

24 slices Canadian bacon

One 450-g can grape leaves in brine, drained and rinsed

1 Wash and dry the quail, then season generously with the black pepper. Wrap three strips of bacon around each bird and then wrap with a grape leaf, securing with a piece of soaked twine. The birds may be prepared ahead of time, covered and refrigerated until needed.

2 Grill the quail over medium-hot heat, turning frequently, about 15 to 20 minutes. Unless you have a large grill, you'll probably have to cook the quail in two batches.

Serves 4

Grilled quail

Be careful not to cook these delicate little birds for too long, or they'll get tough. When cooked just right, they are truly succulent.

1 tbsp crushed garlic

Juice of 1 lemon

50 ml/¼ cup dry vermouth

1 tbsp juniper berries, smashed

½ tsp dried thyme leaves

2 tsp rubbed sage

Salt and pepper, to taste

2 tbsp olive oil

Six 100 to 125-g quails, split open at the backbone to lie flat

1 Combine all the ingredients except the quail and mix well.

2 Place the quail in a glass baking dish. Pour the marinade over the quail, turning to make sure both sides are coated. Cover and refrigerate for 1 to 4 hours, or overnight.

3 Grill over medium-hot heat, skin side down, for 8 to 10 minutes. Turn and cook about 5 to 6 minutes more or until the juices run clear.

Serves 6

Poussins with lemon-coriander marinade

When I prepare these birds for guests, I often pair them with wild rice pilaf and some greens. For some people, half a bird is just enough, but for big eaters like me, I serve one whole poussin per person.

Two 700-g poussins, halved (ask your butcher to do this)

2 tsp ground coriander

1 tsp ground turmeric

125 ml/½ cup fresh lemon juice

50 ml/¼ cup olive oil

3 tbsp finely chopped coriander

2 cloves garlic, crushed

2 whole spring onions, sliced thinly

2 tbsp garlic salt

2 tsp freshly ground black pepper

1 Rinse the poussins with cold water and pat dry with kitchen paper. Combine the coriander and turmeric, blend well and rub the poussins with the mixture. Set aside.

2 Combine the remaining ingredients, except the garlic salt and pepper, in a medium bowl.

3 Place the poussins in a large glass baking dish. Pour the marinade over the poussins, turning to make sure all sides are coated. Cover and marinate in the refrigerator for 4 to 6 hours, or overnight.

4 Remove the poussins, reserving the marinade, and blot dry with kitchen paper. Season with garlic salt and pepper. Grill over medium-hot heat, starting skin side down, turning and basting occasionally with the reserved marinade, for 20 to 25 minutes or until the juices run clear.

Serves 2 to 4

Grilled venison steaks

People often make the mistake of overcooking venison and other game. At the most, it should be cooked to medium, or better yet, medium-rare.

125 ml/½ cup Italian salad dressing

125 ml/½ cup soy sauce

2 tbsp spicy mustard

1 tbsp Worcestershire sauce

2 cloves garlic, crushed

Sea salt and freshly ground black pepper

2 venison steaks, 1 cm thick

1 Combine all the marinade ingredients and blend well. Place the steaks and the marinade in a resealable plastic bag, seal and turn to coat. Marinate in the refrigerator for 2 to 4 hours.

2 Grill the venison over hot heat for 3 to 4 minutes per side, just enough to leave some pink in the middle.

Serves 4

Opposite Grilled venison steaks

Barbecued duck breasts and porcini mushrooms

The southwest of France is known for its dishes made with duck, as well as for its abundance of fungi, which are usually eaten together in simple dishes such as this. Begin the meal with a robust vegetable soup, drink a delicious Paulliac or Gaillac and follow with a plate of delectable French cheeses.

4 boned duck breasts, skin on

Sea salt and freshly ground black pepper, to taste

50 ml/¼ cup red wine

5 cloves garlic, chopped

3 tbsp olive oil

700 g porcini mushrooms, or other large mushrooms

2 tbsp chopped parsley

1 Score the skin of the duck evenly, then place in a bowl. Toss with the salt, pepper and half the wine, half the garlic and half the oil. Marinate for at least one hour.

2 Toss the mushrooms with the remaining wine, garlic and oil, and some salt and pepper. These do not need to marinate longer than a few minutes.

3 Grill the duck breasts over hot heat, starting skin side down, about 5 minutes on the skin side and 2 to 3 minutes on the flesh side for medium-rare. As the fat melts and drips off the duck, the skin will become crispy. Meanwhile, grill the mushrooms over hot heat, a few minutes per side.

4 Thinly slice the duck across the grain and serve with the mushrooms and a sprinkling of parsley.

Serves 4

Duck breast with gingery balsamic-orange sauce

Duck – whether wild or domestic – is delicious and tastes best when cooked to medium-rare. This sauce is a perfect complement for the flavourful grilled duck.

1 large duck breast, skinned

125 ml/½ cup fresh orange juice

350 ml/1½ cups chicken stock

50 ml/¼ cup balsamic vinegar

2 tsp grated root ginger

50 g unsalted butter

½ tsp sea salt

1 tsp freshly ground black pepper

1 tsp orange zest

2 tbsp vegetable oil

3 oranges, sliced thickly

1 Rinse the duck and pat dry with kitchen paper. Set aside.

2 Combine the orange juice and chicken stock in a pan over medium-high heat. Bring to the boil and, uncovered, reduce by half, which will take about 15 to 20 minutes. Add the balsamic vinegar and ginger and cook for 2 to 3 minutes more. While constantly whisking, add the butter, 1 tablespoon at a time. After the butter is completely incorporated, add the salt, pepper and zest.

3 Brush the duck breast with the oil. Grill over hot heat. For medium-rare duck, grill 5 to 8 minutes per side, or until done as you desire. Grill the orange slices until they soften and char slightly.

4 Serve the duck on a bed of griddled orange slices, with the sauce poured over.

Serves 2 to 4

Opposite Duck breast with gingery balsamic-orange sauce

Cajun duck with soured cream dressing

Soured cream is a perfect foil for the spiciness of these exciting Cajun seasonings.

4 duck breasts, skinless	1½ tsp ground cumin
3 tbsp olive oil	1 tsp chilli powder
2 cloves garlic, chopped finely	1 tsp sugar
2 small celery stalks, chopped finely	Sea salt and freshly ground black pepper, to taste
1 tbsp ground coriander	350 ml/1½ cups soured cream
1 tbsp dried mixed herbs	4 tbsp snipped fresh chives or chopped coriander

1 Put each duck breast between two sheets of clingfilm. Using a rolling pin, beat and flatten the duck breasts until they are about twice the original size. Lay them in a large glass baking dish.

2 Put the remaining ingredients, except the soured cream and chives, into a blender or food processor and blend until smooth. Pour the mixture over the duck, turning to make sure all sides are coated. Cover and marinate at room temperature for 2 hours, or longer if refrigerated, turning occasionally.

3 Combine the soured cream and chives in a small bowl and mix well. Cover and chill until needed.

4 Transfer the duck to the barbecue and cook over high heat until slightly charred and just cooked through, 2 to 3 minutes per side. Serve immediately with the soured cream mixture.

Serves 4

Duck and apricot skewers

The hearty, sweet flavour of duck is deliciously partnered with the slight acidity of fresh apricots. Make sure the fruit is not overripe, or it will disintegrate during cooking.

4 duck breasts (about 900 g total)	Freshly ground black pepper, to taste
8 firm-ripe fresh apricots	8 flat metal skewers
4 tbsp light soy sauce	
4 tbsp orange marmalade	

1 If necessary, remove the skin from the duck. Cut into chunks and place in a glass baking dish. Halve the apricots and remove their stones.

2 Combine the soy sauce, marmalade and pepper in a small bowl and mix well. Pour the marinade over the duck, cover and marinate at room temperature for 2 hours, or longer in the refrigerator, stirring occasionally.

3 Thread the duck and apricots alternately on to flat metal skewers. Grill over medium-high heat, turning occasionally, 8 to 10 minutes, or until done as you desire.

Serves 4

Opposite Cajun duck with soured cream dressing

Black Forest turkey sandwich

This filling sandwich is good for all sorts of outdoor eating, from a barbecue on the patio to a picnic in the park. Try serving it with German potato salad and a good lager beer.

2 tbsp vegetable oil

225 g shredded red cabbage

2 sharp apples, peeled, cored and chopped

2 tbsp onion salt

1 tsp ground cinnamon

1 tsp freshly ground black pepper

Six 100 to 125-g turkey breasts

12 slices black rye or pumpernickel bread

6 slices Swiss cheese

50 ml/¼ cup mayonnaise

50 ml/¼ cup coarse ground mustard

Olive oil

1 Heat the oil in a large frying pan and add the cabbage and apples. Cook until wilted and tender, about 7 to 10 minutes. Drain well and keep warm.

2 Combine the onion salt, cinnamon and pepper in a small bowl and blend well. In a separate bowl, combine the mayonnaise and mustard and blend well.

3 Season the turkey breasts on both sides with the seasoning mixture and brush them with olive oil. Grill over medium-hot heat for 4 to 5 minutes per side.

4 To serve, spread the mustard mixture on each slice of bread and add some cabbage mixture, a turkey breast, a slice of cheese and top with another slice of bread. Cut each sandwich in half and serve.

Serves 6

Turkey yakitori

These delicious, tender kebabs can be served hot or cold. When skewering the meat, do not push the pieces too close together or the turkey will take longer to cook. Serve with grated daikon radish (mooli) topped with a splash of rice vinegar, and a salad.

FOR THE TURKEY

450 g turkey breast

2 tbsp sake or sherry

2 tbsp light soy sauce

1 tbsp dark soy sauce

2 tbsp orange juice

1 tbsp packed brown sugar

8 wooden skewers, soaked

Olive oil

Spring onions and cucumber, to garnish

FOR THE DIPPING SAUCE

2 tbsp light soy sauce

4 tbsp orange juice

2 spring onions, trimmed and chopped finely

1 small chilli, deseeded and chopped finely

1 Cut the turkey into thin strips and place in a glass baking dish. Combine the sake, soy sauces, orange juice and brown sugar in a small bowl and mix well. Pour the marinade over the turkey, stirring to be sure all the pieces are coated. Cover and marinate in the refrigerator for 30 minutes, stirring occasionally.

2 Drain the turkey and thread the meat onto eight small wooden skewers.

3 Meanwhile, combine all the dipping sauce ingredients in a small bowl and mix well. Set aside to allow the flavours to blend.

4 Lightly brush the turkey skewers with olive oil. Grill over medium heat, turning frequently, 8 to 10 minutes.

5 Garnish with sliced spring onions and cucumber and serve with the dipping sauce.

Serves 4

Above left Black Forest turkey sandwich **right** Turkey yakitori

Spicy-marmalade turkey cutlets

Canned pineapple slices may be substituted – use as many drained rings as you like – but if you're using a fresh pineapple, save the leafy top to use as a garnish for the centre of your serving platter. Serve with a hot or cold rice dish.

1 medium pineapple, cut lengthways into quarters with the rind on, and then scored crossways into 2.5-cm thick slices

1 orange, cut into 1-cm slices

1½ tbsp packed light brown sugar

225 g marmalade

2 tbsp finely chopped spring onions (white and green parts)

½ tsp crushed garlic

½ tsp red pepper sauce

¼ tsp grated root ginger

½ tbsp Worcestershire sauce

½ tbsp vegetable oil

Sea salt and freshly ground black pepper, to taste

Four 1-cm thick turkey cutlets

1 Sprinkle the pineapple and orange slices with the brown sugar.

2 Combine the marmalade, spring onions, garlic, red pepper sauce, ginger, Worcestershire sauce, oil, salt and pepper in a small bowl and mix well.

3 Grill the turkey cutlets and fruit over medium heat, brushing the turkey frequently with the marmalade mixture, turning the turkey and fruit occasionally, about 5 to 7 minutes or until the turkey just loses its pink colour. Serve.

Serves 4

Apple wood-grilled turkey tenderloins

Apple wood on the grill really makes this dish special. It adds an extra smoky sweetness to the natural grill flavours. Beforehand, check that your grill is appropriate for use with wood chips by referring to the manufacturer's instruction manual.

225 g apple wood chips, soaked in water

2 tbsp garlic salt

1 tsp freshly ground black pepper

900 g turkey tenderloins

Olive oil

1 Combine the garlic salt and pepper, blend well and thoroughly season the tenderloins with the mixture. Brush the tenderloins on all sides with olive oil.

2 Add the wood chips to a medium-hot grill. Grill the tenderloins, covered with the grill lid, turning once, for 8 to 9 minutes per side.

3 Remove from the grill and leave to rest for about 5 to 10 minutes before slicing into 1-cm thick medallions to serve.

Serves 4 to 6

MEAT 5

The perfect hamburger

These burgers must of course be served with lettuce, grilled red peppers, mustard, mayonnaise, tomato, relish and ketchup. And don't forget the fries.

450 g minced beef

3 shallots, peeled and chopped finely

1 to 2 tsp horseradish sauce

2 tbsp chopped fresh parsley

Sea salt and freshly ground black pepper, to taste

4 hamburger buns

1 Combine all the ingredients except the buns in a large bowl, mixing with slightly wet hands. Form into four burgers.

2 Grill the burgers over medium heat, 4 to 6 minutes per side or until done as you desire.

3 Meanwhile, split the buns and place them, cut side down, on the grill until toasted. Serve the burgers on the buns, lavishly accompanied with the essential ingredients listed above. Simply perfect.

Serves 4

Barbecued Texan T-bone steaks

For most of us, this recipe would feed a family of four, but in Texas, where outsize appetites are the norm, it will be enough to satisfy two people! Serve with grilled potatoes and asparagus.

2 thick T-bone steaks (about 1.25 kg)

50 ml/¼ cup balsamic vinegar

2 cloves garlic, halved

1 tbsp coarsely ground black pepper

50 g unsalted butter, softened

1 tbsp Dijon mustard

1 tsp Worcestershire sauce

½ tsp fresh lime juice

Sea salt and freshly ground black pepper, to taste

1 Trim the fat from around the steaks.

2 Using a pastry brush, thoroughly coat each steak on both sides with the balsamic vinegar. Rub half a clove of garlic all over both sides of each steak. Season with coarse black pepper, pressing it into the meat. Cover and set aside.

3 Combine the remaining ingredients except the salt and pepper in a small bowl and blend well.

4 Using a pastry brush, brush the sauce all over the steaks. Grill the steaks over medium heat, basting with the sauce after turning, 8 to 10 minutes per side, or longer if you desire. Serve on a warm platter with extra sauce on the side.

Serves 4 to 6

Opposite The perfect hamburger

"Killer" barbecued skirt steak

I've enjoyed this skirt steak recipe more times than I can remember and I'm convinced it gets better each time.

50 ml/¼ cup Worcestershire sauce

50 ml/¼ cup olive oil

2 tbsp bottled steak sauce

4 cloves garlic, crushed

2 tsp fresh lemon juice

1 tsp hot pepper sauce

½ tsp dried mustard

4 tbsp each finely chopped coriander and parsley

One 700 to 900-g skirt steak

1 Combine all the marinade ingredients except the skirt steak and blend well.

2 Trim the meat of all unwanted fat and place in a glass dish. Pour in the marinade. Add the steak to the marinade, coating both sides. Cover and marinate in the refrigerator for 24 hours, turning the meat 4 to 6 times.

3 One hour before cooking, remove the skirt steak from the marinade and pat dry with kitchen paper, reserving the marinade.

4 Grill the steaks over hot heat until done to your liking, basting with the reserved marinade as they cook. For medium, grill for 7 to 8 minutes each side; for well done, 10 minutes will be required. To serve, slice on the bias and across the grain.

Serves 4 to 6

Right Skirt steak with rosemary-orange glaze

Skirt steak with rosemary-orange glaze

Always remember that when grilling skirt steak, you don't want to overcook it. It is tough to start with, which is why it benefits from being marinated overnight. Lightly cooking the meat will help with its tenderness.

225 ml/1 cup teriyaki sauce

125 ml/½ cup fresh orange juice

100 g finely chopped onions

4 cloves garlic, crushed

1 spring onion, thinly sliced (green and white parts)

75 ml/⅓ cup golden syrup

2 tbsp packed dark brown sugar

2 tbsp chopped rosemary

1 tbsp toasted sesame oil

2 tsp sesame seeds

1 tsp crushed red pepper

450 to 900-g skirt steak

1 Combine all the ingredients except the steak in a medium bowl and blend well.

2 Trim the meat of all unwanted fat and place in a glass baking dish. Pour the marinade over the steak, turning to make sure all sides are coated. Cover and marinate in the refrigerator for 24 hours, turning the meat 4 to 6 times.

3 One hour before cooking, remove the skirt steak from the marinade and pat dry with kitchen paper, reserving the marinade.

4 Grill the steak over hot heat until done to your liking, basting with the reserved marinade to create a sweet glaze.

5 To serve, slice on the bias, across the grain. Place the remaining marinade in a saucepan and bring to the boil, then reduce to concentrate the flavours. Serve poured over the sliced meat.

Serves 4 to 6

Flatiron steaks with North African marinade

Flatiron steak is another name for chuck steak. It is a very tasty cut of beef and this North African marinade makes it even better.

1 Spanish onion,
  chopped finely

2 tbsp grated root ginger

4 cloves garlic, crushed

125 ml/½ cup olive oil

75 ml/⅓ cup fresh lemon
  juice

2 tbsp finely chopped
  coriander

2 tbsp soy sauce

1 tbsp dry sherry

1 tbsp chilli powder

2 tsp hot sauce (optional)

2 tsp sea salt

1 tsp ground turmeric

1 tsp ground marjoram

1 tsp freshly ground black
  pepper

4 flatiron steaks (chuck
  steak) (150 to 200 g each)

1 Combine all the ingredients except the steak in a medium bowl and mix well.

2 With a sharp fork, pierce the steaks all over and on both sides. Place the steaks in a resealable plastic bag or shallow glass baking dish, add the marinade and turn to coat. Cover and marinate in the refrigerator overnight, turning the meat occasionally.

3 Before cooking, let the steaks come to room temperature. Because these steaks are somewhat firm and chewy to start with, it is recommended they be cooked medium to medium-rare. Grill over medium-hot heat, 8 to 10 minutes per side. Let the steaks rest, covered loosely with foil, for 5 minutes before serving.

Serves 4

Thai beef kebabs

Remember when using fresh chillies that the heat is not only in the seeds, but also in the membrane to which they are attached. Do not touch any sensitive parts of the body until you have thoroughly washed your hands. To be safe, wear rubber gloves when handling chillies.

FOR THE DIPPING SAUCE

3 tbsp light soy sauce

1 tbsp mirin (sweet rice
  wine) or sherry

1 Thai chilli, deseeded and
  chopped finely

2 spring onions (white and
  green parts), trimmed and
  chopped finely

FOR THE KEBABS

450 g sirloin steak

1 tbsp grated root ginger

2 stalks lemongrass, outer
  leaves removed and
  chopped

1 to 2 Thai chillies, deseeded
  if preferred and chopped

3 cloves garlic, crushed

4 tbsp fresh lime juice

2 tbsp vegetable oil

2 tbsp chopped coriander

8 wooden skewers, soaked

1 Combine the dipping sauce ingredients and set aside to allow the flavours to blend.

2 Trim the steak, cut into long thin strips and place in a glass baking dish. Scatter with the ginger, lemongrass, chilli and garlic. Blend the lime juice and oil and pour over the steak. Cover loosely and marinate in the refrigerator for 30 minutes.

3 Drain the steak and thread onto the skewers. Lightly brush the rack with oil and grill the steak on medium heat for 2 to 4 minutes per side, or until done to your liking.

4 Serve sprinkled with the coriander and accompanied with the dipping sauce.

Serves 4

Above left Flatiron steaks with North African marinade **right** Thai beef kebabs

California tri-tip

Tri-tip is generally considered a treat in California. It uses a special cut of beef – a triangular-shaped, boneless, bottom piece of sirloin. However, I am using the more familiar joint of topside for this recipe.

1.5 to 2.5 kg joint of topside, trimmed

FOR THE SALSA

225-g can chopped tomatoes

1 medium onion, diced

4 tbsp chopped coriander

2 cloves garlic, crushed

2 fresh jalapeño peppers, deseeded and finely chopped

1 tsp ground cumin

Sea salt and freshly ground black pepper

FOR THE RUB

3 tbsp packed light brown sugar

2 tbsp salt

2 tbsp coarsely ground black pepper

2 tbsp dried garlic granules

2 tbsp sweet Hungarian paprika

2 tbsp parsley flakes

2 tbsp dried onion flakes

1 tsp ground cumin

1 tsp cayenne pepper

1 Combine all the salsa ingredients in a medium bowl and blend well. Refrigerate until needed.

2 Combine all the rub ingredients in a small bowl and blend well.

3 Thoroughly season the meat on all sides with the rub.

4 Grill over medium-hot heat for 10 minutes, turn and cook another 10 minutes, repeating the process until the internal temperature reaches 55°C/130°F. Cook longer if desired. To serve, slice the meat thinly across the grain. Top with the salsa.

Serves 6 to 12

Korean beef

In Korea, this dish would be served with kimchi (pickled salty cabbage), stir-fried beansprouts and plain rice. If you can't get kimchi, try a coleslaw or cucumber salad with a vinegar dressing.

1 tbsp sesame seeds

200 g finely chopped spring onions (white and green parts)

2 to 4 cloves garlic, finely chopped

50 ml/¼ cup soy sauce

2 tbsp sugar

2 tbsp dry sherry or sake

2 tbsp groundnut or sesame oil

700 g beef, such as chuck, round, or sirloin

1 Toast the sesame seeds in a heavy frying pan, shaking frequently to avoid burning and popping, until golden. Grind the toasted seeds in a mortar and pestle or spice grinder.

2 Combine the ground sesame seeds with the spring onions, garlic, soy sauce, sugar, sherry and oil in a small bowl and mix well.

3 Slice the meat into strips about 6 mm thick. Place the meat in a glass baking dish. Pour the marinade over the beef, stirring to make sure the pieces are well coated. Marinate for 1 to 2 hours, covered, in the refrigerator.

4 Grill the beef over high heat until browned, but still rare, about 30 seconds to 1 minute per side.

Serves 4 to 6

Sirloin steak with pineapple chutney

With its fruity content in the relish that is served with the steak, this recipe has strong Caribbean connections.

900 g sirloin steak, trimmed of fat

3 tbsp vegetable oil

FOR THE RUB

Sea salt and freshly ground black pepper

1 tsp curry powder

¼ tsp garlic powder

¼ tsp ground ginger

½ tsp allspice

Dash of nutmeg

Dash of cinnamon

FOR THE CHUTNEY

550-g can crushed pineapple, drained

50 g finely chopped spring onions (white and green parts)

50 g flaked coconut, preferably unsweetened

50 g finely chopped red pepper

1 tbsp red pepper sauce

1 tbsp grated root ginger

1 tbsp fresh lime juice

1 tbsp dark rum

Sea salt and white pepper, to taste

1 Combine the rub ingredients in a small bowl and mix well. Transfer the rub to a large sheet of greaseproof paper.

2 Brush both sides of the steak with the oil and roll the steak in it, patting the seasoning into the meat. Set aside.

3 For the chutney, combine all the ingredients in a glass bowl and gently toss. Cover and leave to stand at room temperature until needed.

4 Brush the rack with oil and grill the steak over hot heat, about 8 minutes per side for medium-rare, or until done to your liking. Transfer to a serving platter and serve with the chutney.

Serves 4 to 6

Japanese-style beef skewer

A *hibachi* is required here to capture the full Japanese style. No *hibachi*? Use an ordinary barbecue!

100 g sesame seeds

2 tsp groundnut oil

125 ml/½ cup soy sauce

2 tbsp mirin (sweet rice wine)

1 tbsp caster sugar

1 tbsp instant *dashi* powder

125 ml/½ cup warm water

700 g sirloin steak

4 pieces preserved ginger, sliced

2 spring onions (white and green parts), sliced thinly

8 to 12 metal skewers

1 Dry roast the sesame seeds in a heavy frying pan over medium heat until the seeds are golden brown, being careful not to burn.

2 Place the roasted sesame seeds and the oil in a blender or food processor and blend until a smooth paste is formed.

3 Mix the paste with the soy sauce, mirin, sugar, *dashi* powder and warm water in a small bowl. Cover and refrigerate before use.

4 Cut the beef into 2.5-cm cubes and place in a glass baking dish. Stir the marinade and add it to the meat, stirring to make sure all the pieces are well coated. Cover and marinate in the refrigerator overnight.

5 Remove the beef from dish, reserving the marinade, and thread onto skewers, inserting two slices of preserved ginger between every two cubes of meat.

6 Brush the meat with the reserved marinade and grill over hot heat, about 10 minutes. Continue to brush with the marinade during cooking.

7 To serve, place the skewers on a serving dish and sprinkle with the spring onion.

Serves 4 to 6

Sirloin steaks with apple-horseradish sauce

This apple-horseradish sauce is a good accompaniment for grilled beef. The creaminess of the soured cream in combination with the apple and horseradish makes for a uniquely flavourful sauce.

Four 350-g sirloin steaks

50 ml/¼ cup Worcestershire sauce

FOR THE SAUCE

1 apple, peeled, cored and grated

125 ml/½ cup soured cream or plain yoghurt

50 g fresh horseradish

4 beef stock cubes

1 clove garlic, crushed

FOR THE HERB RUB

Salt and freshly ground black pepper

½ tsp dried thyme

½ tsp dried savory

½ tsp dried marjoram

½ tsp rubbed sage

¼ tsp ground bay leaf

1 Combine all the sauce ingredients in a small bowl and blend well. Set aside.

2 Combine all the herb rub ingredients in a small bowl and blend well.

3 Coat the steaks with the Worcestershire sauce and thoroughly season with the herb rub. Cover and leave to rest 1 to 2 hours.

4 Grill the steaks over medium-hot heat, 7 to 8 minutes per side for medium-rare. Or, cook until done to your liking. Serve with the apple-horseradish sauce.

Serves 4 to 6

Right Glazed sirloin steaks with smoky corn salsa

Glazed sirloin steaks with smoky corn salsa

These steaks are deceptively simple to prepare and will spice up your evening. Don't forget the steak knife!

Six 2.5-cm thick sirloin steaks

Sea salt and freshly ground black pepper

FOR THE SALSA

3 cobs fresh corn, husked

50 g diced red pepper

75 g sliced spring onions (white and green parts)

25 g diced red onion

Juice of 2 limes

2 tbsp jalapeño jelly, or raspberry jam

1 tsp chilli powder

1 tsp sea salt

½ tsp cumin seeds, toasted and ground

1 serrano chilli, deseeded and chopped finely

FOR THE SAUCE

125 ml/½ cup jalapeño jelly, or raspberry jam

125 ml/½ cup ketchup

1 For the salsa, grill the corn cobs quickly over medium-hot heat, turning so they cook and colour evenly, darkening without turning black. When cool enough to handle, cut the kernels from the cobs and place in a medium bowl. Add the red pepper, onions and lime, and gently toss to combine.

2 Combine the jalapeño jelly, or jam, with the chilli powder, salt, cumin and serrano chilli in a separate bowl and whisk to blend. Add the mixture to the vegetables and gently toss to mix. Set aside.

3 For the sauce, combine the jalapeño jelly, or jam, and ketchup in a small pan and simmer 10 to 12 minutes or until the ingredients are incorporated. Set aside.

4 Season the steaks on both sides with the garlic salt and pepper. Grill over medium-hot heat, glazing the steaks with the sauce as you turn them, 5 to 7 minutes per side for medium-rare, or longer if desired. Transfer to plates and serve with the corn salsa.

Serves 6

Lamb chops with Israeli pepper relish

This relish, or salad, from Israel is known as *Horef* and is made with mixed sweet and hot peppers, tomatoes and spices.

Four 2-cm thick lamb loin chops

5 tbsp olive oil

2 green peppers, cut into thick slices

2 mild green chillies, sliced

2 to 3 green chillies, sliced

5 to 7 cloves garlic, chopped

550 g tomatoes, diced, or one 400-g can chopped tomatoes

1 tsp curry powder

Seeds from 2 to 3 cardamom pods or a pinch ground cardamom

Pinch of ground cumin

Pinch of ground turmeric

Pinch of ground ginger

Pinch of sugar, or to taste

Salt and freshly ground black pepper, to taste

Juice of ½ lemon, or to taste

1 For the relish, heat the oil in a frying pan and sauté the peppers, both types of chillies and the garlic until softened, then add the tomato, curry powder and remaining spices except the sugar, salt and pepper. Continue to cook until the mixture thickens.

2 Season with the sugar, salt and pepper, and add the lemon juice. Remove from the heat and chill until needed.

3 Grill the lamb chops over hot heat, 4 to 5 minutes per side. Serve topped with the pepper relish.

Serves 4

Grilled butterflied leg of lamb

Each September, in America, the National Lamb Barbecue Contest is held in Bonner Springs, Kansas. People come from around the world to share their best grilled lamb recipes and one day you just might see me there, entering this recipe.

One 2.25 to 3-kg leg spring lamb, deboned and butterflied (ask your butcher to do this)

8 cloves garlic, sliced thinly

4 tbsp finely chopped rosemary

1 tbsp sea salt

50 ml/¼ cup olive oil

Juice of 2 lemons

2 tsp freshly ground black pepper

3 sprigs fresh rosemary

1 Combine all the ingredients except the lamb in a small bowl.

2 Rub the marinade all over the lamb. Place in a glass baking dish or resealable plastic bag and let the lamb marinate in the refrigerator for 2 to 4 hours, or overnight.

3 Remove the lamb from the refrigerator 30 minutes before grilling.

4 Begin grilling over hot heat to sear the lamb, 5 to 7 minutes per side. Depending upon the type of grill you are using, either turn the grill down to medium-hot, or spread out the coals so your fire cools to medium-hot. Grill the lamb for 30 to 40 minutes, covered if your grill has a lid, turning often. For medium-rare, cook until the internal temperature reaches 55 to 58°C/130 to 135°F. Or, cook until done to your liking. Serve with fresh rosemary sprigs as garnish.

Serves 8 to 10

Opposite Grilled butterflied leg of lamb

Crispy lamb ribs

Although lamb is growing in popularity, you may have difficulty finding whole breasts of lamb in the supermarket. Instead, you can ask your butcher for breasts of lamb already cut into individual pieces.

2 breasts of lamb (about 1.25 kg)

Grated zest and juice 1 lemon

2 cloves garlic, crushed

2 tsp dried marjoram

2 tsp tomato purée

1 tsp packed brown sugar

Pinch cayenne pepper

¼ tsp sea salt

2 tbsp water

1 Trim large areas of fat off the lamb. Cut the breast into ribs (or pairs of ribs). Alternatively, ask the butcher to cut the meat up for you. Place the ribs in a bowl.

2 Mix the remaining ingredients. Pour the marinade over the ribs, turning to make sure they are well coated. Cover and marinate in the refrigerator for 2 to 4 hours.

3 Grill the lamb over medium heat, covered, turning frequently, 10 to 15 minutes, or until well browned.

Serves 4

Right Café la Paz lamb sausage

Café la Paz lamb sausage

For those who have never made sausage, I recommend trying it. Sausage is really nothing more than seasoned chopped meat. This particular sausage has a character all its own and a great sounding name with no meaning – I just liked the sound of it! If you like lamb, you will certainly enjoy this dish. Accompany it with sweet potato mash.

1.25 kg minced lamb

2 tbsp olive oil

2 tbsp sweet Hungarian paprika

1 tbsp sea salt

2 tsp ground cumin, toasted

2 tsp ground coriander, toasted

1 tsp garlic granules

1 tsp crushed red pepper

1 tsp lemon zest

1 tsp fennel seeds

½ tsp freshly ground black pepper

50 ml/¼ cup red wine

3 tbsp finely chopped coriander, to garnish

1 Combine all the ingredients in a large bowl and blend well, working the mixture until it gets sticky.

2 With clean, cool hands, form the mixture into patties or roll into a loaf or log. Sausage is best the day after you make it, so refrigerate for 24 hours.

3 Grill over medium heat, 5 to 7 minutes per side, or until done. Serve garnished with chopped coriander.

Serves 4 to 6

Loin of lamb with walnut-onion chutney

This is a cross between a traditional chutney and an onion marmalade and combines the crunch of nuts with a fruity onion base. This cut of lamb is special when served with the chutney.

1 kg onions, sliced thinly

4 tbsp olive oil

450 g apples, peeled, cored and chopped

225 ml/1 cup red wine

225 g sugar

Sea salt and freshly ground black pepper

75 ml/⅓ cup red wine vinegar

225 g chopped walnuts

Fresh lemon juice, to taste

1.25 kg boneless loin of lamb

1 For the walnut-onion chutney, heat the oil in a large, deep frying pan and cook the onions until well softened, about 10 minutes.

2 Add the apples and red wine and simmer until both the onions and apples are well cooked, about 20 minutes.

3 Stir in the sugar, salt, pepper and vinegar and cook for another 30 minutes until the chutney is thickened and most of the liquid has been absorbed.

4 Add the walnuts and lemon juice and stir them evenly throughout the mixture. Continue cooking for another 10 minutes until all the liquid has gone. Remove from the heat and set aside.

5 Grill the lamb over medium heat, covered, 25 minutes per pound for well done or 22 minutes per pound for medium, or until the internal temperature reaches 75°C/170°F for well-done, 70°C/160°F for medium. Serve with the walnut-onion chutney. The leftover chutney can be kept refrigerated in an airtight container for 3 to 4 weeks.

Serves 4 to 6

Green peppercorn and mustard lamb steaks

A spicy mustard paste is spread thickly over the lamb steaks, giving them a real flavour lift.

1 tbsp green peppercorns, chopped finely

4 tbsp whole-grain mustard

3 tbsp chopped spring onion (white and green parts)

25 g fresh breadcrumbs

3 tbsp chopped fresh parsley

¼ tsp cayenne pepper

1 to 1½ tbsp vegetable oil

Four 2.5-cm thick lamb steaks

1 Put the peppercorns, mustard, spring onions, breadcrumbs, parsley and cayenne pepper in a bowl and mix well. Stir in a bit of oil at a time, just enough to help make a thick paste.

2 Spread the paste on both sides of the lamb steaks and place in a glass baking dish. Cover and marinate at room temperature for 2 hours, or refrigerate for up to 24 hours.

3 Grill the lamb steaks over medium heat 6 to 8 minutes per side, or until done to your liking.

Serves 4

Opposite Green peppercorn and mustard lamb steaks

Skewered lamb with redcurrant coulis

Lamb and redcurrants are a delicious combination of flavours. Redcurrants are only in season for a short time, so it's worth freezing some when they are available, to use out of season.

450 g lean lamb, such as leg or loin chops, cubed

2 tbsp redcurrant jelly

3 tbsp raspberry vinegar

2 tsp soy sauce

2 tbsp vegetable oil

8 fresh rosemary sprigs or wooden skewers, soaked

FOR THE COULIS

75 g fresh redcurrants, rinsed

2 to 3 sprigs fresh mint

1 to 2 tbsp packed brown sugar, or to taste

1 tbsp raspberry vinegar

1 Place the cubed lamb in a glass baking dish. Heat the redcurrant jelly with the vinegar, soy sauce and oil and stir until blended. Pour the marinade over the lamb, stirring to be sure the pieces are well coated. Cover and refrigerate 30 minutes, occasionally spooning the marinade over the lamb.

2 Shred the leaves from the bottom of the sprigs of rosemary and when ready to cook, drain the lamb and thread onto the rosemary sprigs. Alternatively, use wooden skewers.

3 Meanwhile, make the coulis by cooking the redcurrants with the mint sprigs, brown sugar and vinegar over medium-low heat. Simmer for 10 minutes or until tender. Pass through a fine sieve to form a smooth sauce. Set aside.

4 Grill the lamb skewers over medium heat, 3 to 5 minutes per side or until done to your liking. Serve with the coulis.

Serves 4

Lamb burgers with curried cucumber

If you like regular hamburgers, then you will really like lamb burgers. The curried cucumber brings alive the flavours in the lamb. As a variation, try using a combination of minced lamb and minced beef.

FOR THE CURRIED CUCUMBER

1 cucumber, halved lengthways, deseeded and sliced thinly

75 ml/$\frac{1}{3}$ cup plain yoghurt

2 tsp fresh lemon juice

2 tsp honey

$\frac{1}{2}$ to 1 tsp curry powder

Sea salt and freshly ground black pepper

FOR THE BURGERS

700 g minced lamb

2 tsp salt

1 tsp freshly ground black pepper

4 wedges focaccia bread

2 tbsp olive oil

1 red leaf lettuce

1 For the curried cucumber, combine all the ingredients except the cucumber and mix well. Add the dressing to the cucumber and gently mix. Set aside until needed.

2 Place the lamb in a bowl and season with the salt and pepper.

3 Form into four burgers each about 2.5 cm thick. Grill the burgers over medium-hot heat, 5 to 7 minutes per side for medium-rare, or longer if desired.

4 Meanwhile, split the focaccia wedges in half and brush with oil. Toast on the grill while the burgers are cooking until the bread is golden brown, about 35 to 45 seconds.

5 To assemble, top each half of bread with a burger, lettuce leaves, some curried cucumber and another piece of bread. Serve hot.

Serves 4

Above left Skewered lamb with redcurrant coulis **right** Lamb burgers with curried cucumber

Small spicy Moorish kebabs

Kebabs of one kind or another are eaten and enjoyed all over the world. Almost every culture has a version of skewered meat cooked over a fire.

2 cloves garlic, chopped finely	Freshly ground black pepper
2 tsp sea salt	3 tbsp olive oil
1 tsp curry powder	1 tbsp fresh lemon juice
½ tsp coriander seeds	450 g lean pork, cut into small cubes
1 tsp paprika	6 bamboo skewers, soaked
¼ tsp dried thyme	Lime wedges

1 Crush the chopped garlic with the salt using a mortar and pestle.

2 Work the curry powder, coriander seeds, paprika, thyme, black pepper, oil and lemon juice into the garlic and salt. Transfer to a shallow dish and set aside.

3 Remove any excess fat from the pork and chop into small, bite-sized cubes. Skewer the meat, three to four cubes to a stick, and turn the kebabs in the marinade to coat thoroughly. Leave to marinate for a few hours – the longer you leave them, the better the flavour.

4 Cook over high heat until the meat is browned on the outside and cooked through, about 3 to 5 minutes each side, 12 to 20 minutes in total.

5 Serve immediately with lime wedges.

Serves 3 to 4

Indonesian pork brochettes

Coconut, ginger, chillies and lime give a distinctly Asian flavour to these pork skewers. You could use cubes of chicken or prawns (shrimp) instead if you prefer.

225 ml/1 cup coconut milk	Salt and freshly ground black pepper
6 spring onions (white and green parts)	Generous pinch of ground turmeric
2 cloves garlic	800 g lean pork, cubed
2 fresh red chillies, halved and deseeded	Six metal skewers
5-cm piece root ginger, peeled and chopped	Lime wedges
Grated zest and juice of 2 small limes	

1 Place all the ingredients except the pork and lime wedges into a blender or food processor and purée until the mixture is almost smooth.

2 Put the pork in a glass baking dish. Pour the coconut mixture over the pork, stirring to make sure the pieces are well coated. Cover and leave to marinate in the refrigerator about 2 hours, stirring occasionally.

3 Thread the pork cubes onto six skewers and brush with any remaining coconut mixture.

4 Grill over medium heat, turning frequently, for about 12 to 20 minutes. Serve with noodles and garnished with lime wedges.

Serves 4

Opposite Indonesian pork brochettes

Pork chops with onion and lemongrass stuffing

Grilling these delicious chops gives a crisp outside texture to the meat, while he inside stuffing holds the surprise flavour of lemongrass.

FOR THE STUFFING

2 large red onions, chopped finely

2 tbsp groundnut oil

Pinch chilli powder

2 stalks lemongrass, bruised and chopped finely

150 g fresh breadcrumbs

2 big handfuls coriander, chopped, plus more for garnish

Sea salt and freshly ground black pepper, to taste

1 large egg, beaten

4 tbsp unsalted butter, melted

Four 140 to 170-g pork chops

1 To make the stuffing, preheat the oven to 200°C/400°F/Gas Mark 6.

2 Heat the oil in a frying pan and cook the onion, chilli and lemongrass for 8 to 10 minutes or until well softened. Remove from the heat and let cool slightly.

3 Mix the breadcrumbs with the coriander, salt and pepper in a large bowl. Add the onion mixture and blend well. Add the beaten egg, then mix to bind the stuffing. Add a little melted butter if necessary to keep the mixture together.

4 Trim the pork chops of excess fat. Make an incision in each of the chops to create a pocket into which the stuffing can be inserted. Press small balls of stuffing into the pockets.

5 Grill the pork chops over hot heat, 10 minutes per side. Serve topped with a stuffing ball and garnish with chopped coriander.

Serves 4

Peurco adobo

These will probably be the best pork chops you will ever eat.

Four 2.5-cm thick pork loin chops

350-g jar jalapeño peppers, undrained

2 tsp dried oregano

4 cloves garlic, crushed

2 tsp ground cumin

50 ml/¼ cup cider vinegar

1 Combine all the ingredients except the pork chops in a blender with a steel blade. Purée.

2 Place the chops in a glass dish. Pour the purée over the pork chops and marinate in the refrigerator for 4 hours, or overnight.

3 Grill over medium-hot heat, 5 to 7 minutes per side. Or, cook until done to your liking.

Serves 4

Opposite Pork chops with onion and lemongrass stuffing

Guava-glazed baby ribs

Ribs are particularly well suited to fruit-based sauces and these Caribbean-inspired ribs are no exception.

4 racks baby back pork ribs
(450 to 900 g each)

¼ tsp ground cloves

⅛ tsp mace

FOR THE ISLAND RUB

50 g packed brown sugar

50 g sugar

2 tbsp seasoned salt

2 tbsp garlic salt

2 tbsp celery salt

2 tbsp chilli powder

2 tbsp freshly ground
black pepper

1 tsp allspice

1 tsp ground ginger

½ tsp cayenne pepper

FOR THE GLAZE

225 ml/1 cup guava paste or
fruit purée, such as mango
or plum

50 ml/¼ cup honey

50 ml/¼ cup fresh orange juice

2 tbsp soy sauce

2 tbsp fresh lime juice

1 tsp ground ginger

½ tsp ground allspice

1 tsp sea salt

½ tsp white pepper

1 Combine the rub ingredients in a medium bowl and blend well. Place in an airtight container and set aside.

2 Combine the glaze ingredients in a small saucepan and cook over medium-low heat, stirring with a whisk. Cook for about 10 minutes until the ingredients have been incorporated. Set aside.

3 Remove the membrane from the back of the ribs. Sprinkle both sides of each rack with the rub. Grill the ribs over medium heat, meat side down, covered, for 4 to 6 hours, turning after 2 hours then again 1 hour later.

4 To test for doneness, take two side-by-side ribs and if they tear apart easily, they are about done. Using a pastry brush, coat each slab on both sides with the glaze, cook for 10 to 15 minutes, then repeat the process.

5 Allow the ribs to rest for 10 to 15 minutes before cutting into pieces to serve.

Serves 8 to 10

Grilled veal chops

This recipe is for all of the "grilling gourmets" out there. It is fantastic with a good Merlot. Panko breadcrumbs, which are Japanese, create a crunchier crust than ordinary breadcrumbs and can be purchased in Asian markets.

4 veal chops (cut so the bone is exposed - ask your butcher to do this)

2 tbsp garlic salt

2 tsp freshly ground black pepper

2 cups panko breadcrumbs

125 ml/½ cup olive oil

1 tbsp crushed garlic

8 thin slices prosciutto

4 wedges soft blue-veined cheese

1 Season the chops with the garlic salt and pepper.

2 Grill the chops over hot heat, 7 to 9 minutes per side or until done to your liking.

3 Combine the breadcrumbs, oil and garlic. Top each chop with two slices of prosciutto and a wedge of cheese. Spoon the breadcrumb mixture on top of the cheese. Place on the grill, cover and cook about 10 minutes or until the cheese melts. Serve hot.

Serves 4

Country-style pork ribs

Ribs are one of the original finger foods, so don't be shy when eating with your hands - grab hold of a rib and take a nice, big bite. Wash it down with some homemade lemonade.

900 g pork ribs

50 g packed brown sugar

2 tbsp sweet Hungarian paprika

1 tbsp sea salt

2 tsp garlic granules

1 tsp onion flakes

½ tsp ground celery seed

½ tsp cayenne pepper

1 Combine all the ingredients except the ribs in a small bowl and mix well.

2 Trim any excess fat from the ribs and thoroughly season with the rub.

3 Grill the ribs over medium heat, covered, turning every 10 minutes, about 30 to 45 minutes.

Serves 4

Opposite Country-style pork ribs

Grilled carne adovada

The title of this recipe roughly translates to "chilli pork". The 24 chillies make it really hot, even without the chilli seeds. It's about the level of heat as Tabasco. The marinade can be made up as a sauce which is good as a topping for omelets and would satisfy most chilli heads.

900 g pork tenderloin

24 dried red chilli peppers

2 tbsp bacon fat

250 g diced onions

4 cloves garlic, crushed

2 tbsp plain flour

1 tsp sea salt

½ tsp ground Mexican oregano

225ml/1 cup tomato juice

Soured cream and lime wedges, to garnish

1 Wash the chillies and remove the stems and seeds. Place them in a saucepan, cover with water and boil for 30 minutes. Drain and put the softened chillies through a food mill.

2 Heat the bacon fat in a frying pan and sauté the onions and garlic. Add the flour and stir to make a smooth paste. Add the chilli pulp, salt, oregano and tomato juice and simmer, stirring occasionally, for 30 minutes.

3 Slice the tenderloin into 1-cm thick fillets. Place in a glass dish. Marinate in the red chilli sauce in the refrigerator overnight.

4 Grill the meat over medium-hot heat, 5 to 7 minutes per side, or until done to your liking. Serve with eggs or in a flour tortilla (like a soft taco), garnished with soured cream and lime wedges.

Serves 4

Cuban pork tenderloin with mojo marinade

This is my "uncle" Fidel Castro's favourite meal. Why do I call him my uncle? It's because we share the same birthday!

2 pork tenderloins, trimmed (700 g each)

125 ml/½ cup fresh orange juice

50 ml/¼ cup fresh lime juice

8 cloves garlic, crushed

1½ tbsp sea salt

1 tbsp ground cumin

1 tbsp ground coriander

1 tbsp sugar

Half a habanero chilli, or 1 jalapeño pepper, deseeded and chopped finely

1 Combine all the ingredients except the pork in a medium bowl and blend well.

2 Place the tenderloins and the marinade in a resealable plastic bag, seal and turn to coat. Marinate in the refrigerator for 4 to 6 hours, or overnight.

3 Grill the tenderloins over medium heat, turning every 7 to 10 minutes, for 35 to 45 minutes total. Cook until the internal temperature reaches 63 to 73°C/145 to 165°F, being careful not to overcook.

Serves 4 to 6

Opposite Grilled carne adovada

Japanese ginger pork chops

Heat up the sake when these chops are ready to be served. They go well with fried rice or egg noodles.

4 pork chops

50 ml/¼ cup soy sauce

2 tbsp grated root ginger

2 tbsp mirin (sweet rice wine)

1 Combine all the ingredients except the pork chops and blend well.

2 Place the pork in a glass dish. Pour the mixture over the pork chops and marinate for 2 to 4 hours. Remove from the marinade.

3 Grill over medium-hot heat, 5 to 7 minutes per side, being careful not to overcook and dry out the pork chops.

Serves 4

Curry mango pork chops

No plain-Jane pork chops these. This is a spicy-fruity main dish best served with simple side dishes, such as basmati rice or black beans. A spinach salad will add contrasting colour and texture.

Six 2.5-cm thick lean pork chops

FOR THE CURRIED MANGO

2 mangoes, cut into bite-sized chunks

2 tbsp unsalted butter, melted

50 g packed brown sugar

1 to 1 ½ tsp curry powder

FOR THE PORK CHOPS

1½ tsp grated root ginger

3 cloves garlic, crushed

125 ml/½ cup dry sherry or dry wine

125 ml/½ cup ginger or orange marmalade

50 ml/¼ cup soy sauce

2 tbsp light sesame oil

1 To make the curried mango, preheat the oven to 180°C/350°F/Gas Mark 4. Place the drained mango in a baking dish or pie plate. Combine the butter, sugar and curry powder and spoon over the fruit. Bake in the oven for 30 minutes. Set aside and keep warm until needed.

2 For the pork chops, take the point of a knife and make six shallow incisions on each side of the chops. Make a paste with the ginger and garlic and rub it into the meat on both sides, spreading any remaining paste on top of the chops. Set aside.

3 Combine the sherry, marmalade, soy sauce and sesame oil in a small bowl and mix well. Place the pork chops in a glass dish. Pour the marinade over the pork chops, turning to make sure all sides are coated. Marinate for 30 minutes.

4 Place the chops on the hottest part of the grill and cook, covered, for about 15 minutes, basting occasionally with the marinade and turning 2 or 3 times.

5 Serve, accompanied with the curried mango.

Serves 6

VEGETABLES 6

Feta-stuffed peppers

Here is a unique twist on stuffed peppers. If you don't care for anchovies, leave them out, but eliminate the sugar if you do so.

4 red peppers, halved
  and deseeded

2 medium tomatoes,
  quartered

280 g feta cheese, cut into
  small cubes

50-g can anchovies, drained
  and chopped

280 g black olives, halved
  and stoned

8 tsp sugar

Olive oil

16 fresh basil leaves

1 Place a tomato quarter, some cubes of feta, some chopped anchovy, some olive halves and 1 teaspoon sugar into each pepper half. Drizzle with olive oil and place basil leaves on top.

2 Grill the peppers over medium heat until they are soft and the skin begins to char, about 10 minutes.

Serves 2 to 4

Barbecue-roasted potatoes and onions with olives

These potatoes are a welcome change from the ubiquitous baked potato that seems to be the usual barbecue fare.

700 g potatoes, sliced thinly

2 large onions, sliced thinly

3 tbsp olive oil

1 tbsp white wine vinegar

3 tbsp finely chopped
  thyme or rosemary

Sea salt and freshly ground
  black pepper, to taste

16 stoned black olives

1 Put the potato and onion into a large bowl. Whisk together the oil and vinegar and drizzle over the potato mixture. Toss well. Add the thyme, salt and pepper and toss again until well coated.

2 Divide the mixture between six large squares of thick foil. Slice the olives into thin rings and scatter them over the top.

3 Close the parcels, being sure to secure the seams. Grill the parcels over medium heat, turning occasionally, about 30 minutes, or until the potatoes are tender.

Serves 6

Opposite Feta-stuffed peppers

Grilled Indonesian aubergine

This recipe makes a great vegetarian meal when served with a tossed salad and a crunchy vegetable. As a side dish, it is also a good addition to a meal featuring pork tenderloin.

1 large aubergine (eggplant), cut into 1-cm slices

2 cloves garlic, minced

2 shallots, peeled and chopped finely

1 serrano chilli, deseeded and chopped finely (use rubber gloves when handling chillies)

1 tbsp toasted sesame oil

50 g crunchy peanut butter

1 tbsp soy sauce

1 tbsp packed light brown sugar

1 tbsp fresh lemon juice

225 ml/1 cup water

Salt and pepper, to taste

100 g unsalted butter, melted

2 cloves garlic, crushed

1 Lightly sprinkle the aubergine slices with salt, place in a colander and let drain for about 1 hour. Rinse and pat dry.

2 In a small saucepan, sauté the crushed garlic, shallots and chilli in the sesame oil over medium-low heat, stirring occasionally, until the vegetables are soft but not browned. Add the peanut butter and cook, stirring, for 1 minute. Add the soy sauce, brown sugar, lemon juice and water. Bring to the boil. Reduce until the mixture has slightly thickened. Season to taste with salt and pepper.

3 Combine the melted butter and remaining two cloves of garlic in a small bowl. Brush the aubergine slices with the garlic butter and grill over medium-hot heat 3 to 4 minutes per side or until done. Transfer to a serving plate and top with the sauce.

Serves 4

Middle Eastern grilled aubergine

This dish of thinly sliced, grilled aubergine is served with a sweet-and-sour pomegranate dressing, a leafy green salad and fresh, fragrant mint. It is an excellent accompaniment to grilled chicken or lamb. Pomegranate syrup is available in Middle Eastern markets.

1 large aubergine (eggplant)

3 tbsp olive oil

5 cloves garlic, chopped

4 to 5 tbsp pomegranate syrup or molasses

6 tbsp balsamic vinegar

Handful of mixed salad leaves

Sea salt and freshly ground black pepper,, to taste

3 tbsp finely chopped mint

Pomegranate seeds, to garnish

1 Slice the aubergine and brush the slices with olive oil.

2 Grill the slicest over a medium heat until they are lightly browned and tender. Remove them from the grill and rub with the garlic.

3 Combine the pomegranate syrup with an equal amount of the balsamic vinegar and set aside. Toss the greens with a little oil and the remaining balsamic vinegar, adding salt and pepper as desired.

4 Serve the aubergine slices sprinkled with the pomegranate-vinegar syrup, chopped mint and the pomegranate seeds, with the greens on the side.

Serves 4

Opposite Middle Eastern grilled aubergine

Tofu and tomato kebabs

This dish is delicious when made on a barbecue. For an alternative way of serving, the vegetables and tofu can be nestled in sliced baguettes or wraps.

2 courgettes (zucchini), cut into thin strips

300 g firm tofu, cut into 1-cm cubes

24 cherry tomatoes

2 tbsp olive oil

Sea salt and freshly ground black pepper, to taste

1 tbsp chopped fresh rosemary

1 tbsp chopped fresh parsley

2 bunches rocket, rinsed

8 metal skewers

FOR THE DRESSING

2 tsp wholegrain mustard

3 tbsp olive oil

2 tbsp balsamic vinegar

2 tsp apple juice

1 Wrap the tofu cubes with the courgette strips and then thread the tomatoes and wrapped tofu pieces alternately onto the skewers.

2 Brush with olive oil and sprinkle with the salt, pepper, rosemary and parsley. Grill the kebabs, turning occasionally, for 6 to 8 minutes under a medium heat.

3 For the dressing, mix all the ingredients in a jar and shake well to amalgamate.

4 To serve, lay the rocket on a serving plate, place the kebabs on top and drizzle with the dressing. Alternatively wrap the dressed kebabs and garnish with parsley.

Serves 4

Penne with grilled aubergine and tomatoes

You can put this dinner together in 15 minutes or less, so you'll have plenty of time to eat and enjoy! Or, try it with courgettes or yellow squash as an alternative to aubergine.

1 large aubergine (eggplant), cut into 1-cm slices

450 g tomatoes, each cut in half

Olive oil

Salt and pepper, to taste

225 g penne pasta

2 tbsp chopped parsley

2 tbsp olive oil

4 cloves garlic, crushed

40 g freshly grated Parmesan

1 Brush both sides of the aubergine slices and tomato halves with olive oil. Season to taste with salt and pepper. Grill the vegetables over medium heat – the aubergine about 3 to 4 minutes per side or until tender and the tomatoes until charred, turning occasionally, about 6 to 7 minutes. Leave to cool.

2 Meanwhile, cook the pasta in a large pot of boiling, salted water until tender but still firm (al dente). Drain the pasta and return it to the same pot.

3 Cut the aubergine into strips and the tomatoes into bite-sized pieces.

4 Add the aubergine, tomatoes, parsley, olive oil and garlic to the pasta and toss to blend. Sprinkle with the cheese, season with salt and pepper and serve immediately.

Serves 4

Opposite Tofu and tomato kebabs

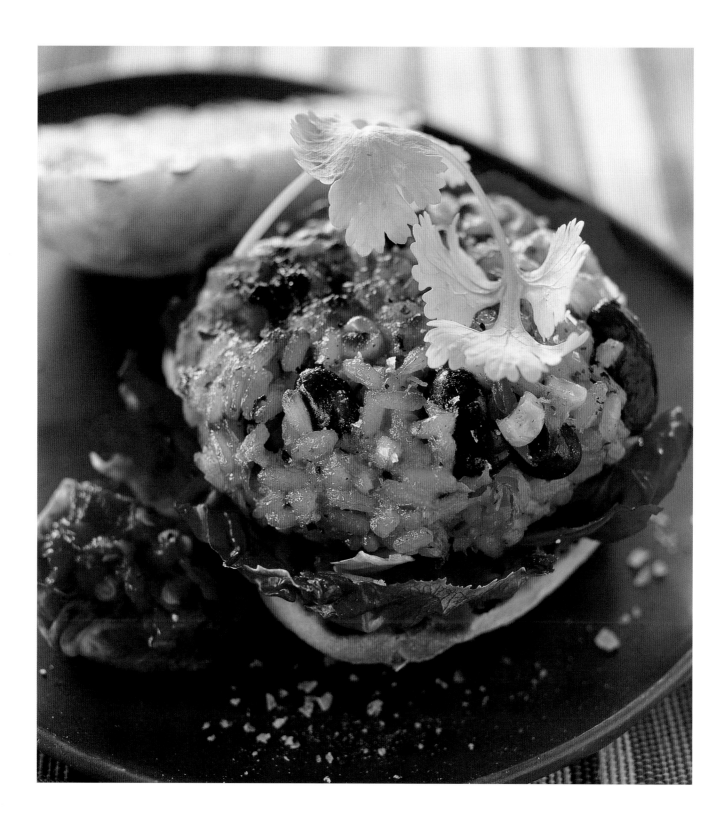

Chilli-rice burgers

These burgers can be grilled on the barbecue, but it is a good idea to put them in a grill basket so they can be easily turned over.

3 tbsp olive oil

2 cloves garlic, crushed

4 red chillies, deseeded and chopped

40 g short-grain rice, uncooked

1 large carrot, grated

2 tbsp tomato purée mixed with 2 tbsp water

550 ml/2½ cups vegetable stock, plus 1 to 2 tbsp

Sea salt and freshly ground black pepper, to taste

225 g canned kidney beans, drained

100 g corn kernels

2 tbsp chopped coriander

1 large tomato, sliced

6 buns, lightly toasted

Chilli pepper relish, to serve

1 Heat 2 tablespoons oil in a frying pan and sauté the garlic and chilli for 5 minutes. Stir in the rice and continue to cook for 3 minutes, stirring occasionally. Stir in the carrot.

2 Add the tomato purée mixture, vegetable stock, salt and pepper to the frying pan. Bring to the boil. Reduce the heat and simmer for 20 minutes, or until the rice is cooked, stirring occasionally and adding a little extra stock if necessary.

3 Add the kidney beans and corn. Cook for another 5 minutes or until the mixture is very stiff and will stick together. Stir in the coriander and remove from the heat. Leave to cool.

4 When the mixture is cool enough to handle, wet your hands slightly and shape the mixture into six large burgers. Cover and refrigerate for at least 30 minutes.

5 Brush the burgers with olive oil and grill over medium heat for 4 to 5 minutes, turn carefully and cook another 3 to 4 minutes or until heated through. To serve, place the burgers on the buns and top with a little chilli pepper relish.

Serves 6

Grilled portobello and watercress burgers

Some people think portobellos are the "fillet steak" of mushrooms because of their meaty texture. I like to grill them and serve them as an entrée, vegetable or an accompaniment.

125 ml/½ cup mayonnaise

1 tbsp Dijon mustard

2 tsp finely chopped rosemary

3 cloves garlic, crushed

3 tbsp olive oil

4 large portobello mushrooms, stems trimmed

Salt and pepper, to taste

4 wholewheat buns, toasted

2 bunches watercress

1 Mix the mayonnaise, mustard, rosemary and 1 crushed garlic clove in a bowl and blend well. Cover and refrigerate until needed.

2 Combine the oil and 2 crushed garlic cloves in a small bowl and blend well. Thoroughly brush the mushroom caps with the garlic oil and season to taste with salt and pepper. Grill over medium-hot heat 8 to 10 minutes per side, being careful not to let them burn.

3 To serve, spread both sides of the toasted buns with the mayonnaise mixture. Place some watercress on the bottom of the bun, add a mushroom cap and top with the other slice of the bun.

Serves 4

Opposite Chilli-rice burgers

Courgettes with black olives and mint

A simply delicious accompaniment to seafood and fish, this Mediterranean-inspired dish is even good with a burger.

8 black olives, such as kalamata

3 large courgettes (zucchini), green and yellow varieties

Sea salt and finely ground black pepper

2 tbsp olive oil

3 tbsp coarsely chopped mint

2 tsp fresh lemon juice

1 Stone and thinly slice the olives. Cut the courgettes diagonally into 6-mm thick slices. Place in a bowl with the salt, pepper and olive oil. Toss to coat.

2 Grill the courgettes over medium-hot heat until lightly charred and just tender, about 3 to 4 minutes per side. Transfer to a bowl and toss with the olives, mint and lemon juice.

Serves 4

Courgettes and sweet onion brochettes

The seasoning caramelises a little during cooking, giving the vegetables a slightly sweet accent, which is totally irresistible.

3 tbsp olive oil

3 tbsp tomato purée

3 tbsp finely chopped fresh rosemary

1 tbsp sugar

24 small onions, peeled

6 courgettes (zucchini), each cut into 4 pieces

6 metal skewers

1 Combine the oil, tomato purée, rosemary and sugar in a small bowl and mix well.

2 Put the onions and courgettes in a resealable plastic bag, add the tomato mixture, seal and turn to coat. Marinate for about 30 minutes.

3 Alternately thread the onions and courgettes onto six metal skewers. Grill over medium-high heat, turning occasionally, until slightly blackened and just cooked through, about 15 minutes.

Serves 6

Squash and apples with brown sugar

Here, wedges of squash and apples are baked in foil, with butter and brown sugar enhancing their natural sweet flavour and luscious texture.

1 small acorn squash

2 sharp apples, such as Bramleys

6 tbsp unsalted butter

50 g packed light brown sugar

Juice of 1 lemon

Sea salt and ground pepper, to taste

Allspice, to taste

3 tbsp finely chopped parsley

1 Halve the squash lengthways. Scoop out and discard the seeds and membranes. Cut each half into 3 wedges.

2 Cut the apples in half and then each half into thirds. Core each wedge.

3 Place the squash and apple wedges on a large sheet of thick foil and top with tablespoons of butter and brown sugar. Sprinkle with the lemon juice, salt, pepper, allspice and parsley.

4 Close the parcel, being sure to secure the seams. Grill over medium heat, turning the parcel frequently, until the squash is tender, about 40 minutes.

Serves 6

Opposite Courgettes with black olives and mint

Halloumi with brandy and lemon-herb marinade

Grilled halloumi cheese is one of the great pleasures of eating in Cyprus. When cold, halloumi is rubbery, slightly tough and quite salty; when heated over a grill, it grows soft and supple, imbued with the wonderful smoky scent of the fire. Halloumi can be found in Middle Eastern grocery stores or markets.

225 g halloumi cheese, cut into 6-mm slices

2 tbsp olive oil

2 tbsp brandy

Several pinches of *herbes de Provence* or *bouquet garni*

1 clove garlic, crushed

1 lemon, cut in half

1 Combine the cheese with the olive oil, brandy, herbs, garlic and juice of one lemon half. Marinate for 30 minutes, or up to several hours in the refrigerator.

2 Cut the remaining lemon into wedges and set aside.

3 Grill the halloumi cheese quickly over hot heat, letting it brown lightly on each side, but being careful that it doesn't melt through the rack.

4 Remove the cheese from the hot fire, garnish with the lemon wedges and serve immediately.

Serves 4

Centre Halloumi with brandy and lemon-herb marinade

Chinese long beans with cracked black pepper

These beans, also known as yard-long beans, can be found in Asian markets and in some well-stocked supermarkets. They are good with everything from grilled steak and potatoes to fried chicken. Use of a grill basket when grilling the beans would make turning simple.

1 medium red pepper

2 tbsp olive oil

1 medium onion, cut into 1-cm slices

450 g Chinese long beans or green beans, trimmed

2 tbsp soy sauce

1 tbsp water

2 tsp sugar

1 to 2 tsp cracked black pepper (crushed, not ground)

1 Rub the red pepper with olive oil and grill over medium-hot heat, turning, until charred all over. This will take 10 to 15 minutes. Place in a paper bag and set aside.

2 Brush both sides of the onion slices with olive oil and grill until soft and charred, about 4 to 5 minutes per side, or until done to your liking. Set aside and keep warm.

3 Combine the soy sauce, water, sugar and cracked black pepper in a small bowl and blend well.

4 Grill the beans over medium-hot heat, turning as needed, until tender-crisp, 6 to 7 minutes.

5 Place the beans in a serving bowl. Remove the pepper from the bag and peel, discarding the seeds and membranes. Chop and add to the beans. Chop the onions and add to the beans. Pour in the sauce and gently toss. Serve warm.

Serves 4 to 5

Nine-spice grilled vegetables

If you think this seasoning is good with vegetables, try it on your next pork loin. You won't be disappointed.

3 tbsp light brown sugar, dried*

3 tbsp seasoned salt

2 tbsp sweet Hungarian paprika

1 tbsp chilli powder

1 tbsp black pepper

2 tsp garlic granules or garlic powder

1 tsp onion granules

1 tsp dried basil

1 tsp cayenne

Olive oil

A combination of your favourite vegetables, such as courgettes (zucchini), yellow squash, peppers (red, green or yellow), onions, mushrooms, potatoes or sweet potatoes

1 Combine all the ingredients except the olive oil and the vegetables in a small bowl and blend well.

2 Cut all the vegetables into pieces roughly the same size, all about 1 cm thick. Brush with the olive oil and sprinkle generously with the spice mixture. Grill over medium-hot heat until just cooked through, turning occasionally – most vegetables will be cooked in about 6 to 7 minutes. Parboil or bake the potatoes and sweet potatoes before grilling for this timetable.

* To make dry brown sugar, spread the sugar out on a baking sheet and leave to air-dry for 2 to 3 hours, then sieve to break up the clumps.

Makes 70 g spice

Vegetable gyros with tzatziki sauce

Although I'm a proud meat-eater, this is one of my favourite sandwiches – it's healthy and tasty, not to mention filling and satisfying.

FOR THE FILLING

Four 2-cm thick slices firm tofu, well drained

1 green pepper, deseeded and cut into 8 strips

1 red pepper, deseeded and cut into 8 strips

8 spring onions, left whole with all but 3 in green tops trimmed

125 ml/½ cup bottled Italian salad dressing

2 tbsp finely chopped mint

4 pitta bread

2 plum tomatoes, sliced thinly

50 g crumbled cheese

FOR THE TZATZIKI SAUCE

225 ml/1 cup yoghurt or soured cream

½ cucumber, peeled, deseeded and diced

4 cloves garlic, crushed

½ tsp sea salt

¼ tsp white pepper

1 Place the tofu, peppers and spring onions in a glass baking dish. Combine the dressing and mint in a small bowl and mix well. Pour the marinade over the tofu and vegetables, making sure they are well coated. Cover and set aside for 15 minutes.

2 Combine all the tzatziki sauce ingredients in a small bowl and blend well. Cover and refrigerate until needed.

3 Grill the tofu and vegetables over medium heat, basting with the marinade and turning as needed, until lightly charred, about 5 minutes. Remove from the grill and set aside, keeping them warm. Grill the pitta bread, turning several times until warm.

4 To assemble the gyro, place the tofu in the middle of the pitta bread and top with a slice of red and green pepper, two spring onions, tomato, cheese and the sauce. Roll up the sandwich and secure with cocktail sticks. Serve immediately.

Serves 4

Opposite Vegetable gyros with tzatziki sauce

VEGETABLES

Pesto and mozzarella sub

I love making these sandwiches for picnics - they go nicely with a crisp wine and good company. This recipe makes about 150 ml/^{2}/$_3$ cup pesto, which is more than you'll need. Refrigerate the leftovers in an airtight container with a little olive oil poured on top to seal in the colour and flavour.

FOR THE PESTO

8 tbsp fresh basil leaves

3 tbsp walnuts or pine kernels, toasted and chopped

2 cloves garlic, crushed

3 tbsp freshly grated Parmesan

75 ml/^{1}/$_3$ cup olive oil

Salt and pepper, to taste

FOR THE SANDWICH

1 medium onion, cut into 1-cm thick slices

2 peppers, red and yellow, quartered and deseeded

3 small aubergines (eggplants), cut into 6-mm thick slices

One 35-cm long Italian bread roll, cut in half

Olive oil, for brushing vegetables and bread

100 g grated mozzarella cheese

3 tbsp finely shredded basil leaves, to garnish

1 To make the pesto, combine all the ingredients in a food processor or blender and blend until smooth. Cover and chill.

2 Brush the onions, peppers and aubergine with olive oil and grill over medium-hot heat until cooked through, about 4 to 5 minutes per side. Remove the vegetables from the grill and cut the peppers into strips.

3 Brush the cut side of the roll with oil and grill, cut side down, until golden brown and toasted, about 2 to 3 minutes. Spread each piece of roll with 4 tablespoons pesto and divide the vegetables and cheese between each piece. Wrap the bread in foil and place the parcel back on the grill, until the cheese melts, 3 to 4 minutes. Garnish with the basil leaves and slice to serve.

Serves 4

Cheese sausages

These tasty treats aren't called sausages because they contain meat, but because of their sausage-like shape. In fact, these cheesy bites are meat-free.

150 g fresh breadcrumbs	**1 tbsp water**
130 g cheddar cheese, grated	**Sea salt and freshly ground black pepper, to taste**
1 medium onion, chopped	**Olive oil**
2 tbsp chopped parsley	
1 tsp dried mustard	
1 tsp Worcestershire sauce	

1 Place all the ingredients except the salt, pepper and oil in a food processor and process until the mixture forms a soft dough. Add the salt and pepper and process a few seconds more.

2 Divide the mixture into eight portions and shape into "sausages".

3 Brush with olive oil and grill over hot heat, turning until browned all over, about 10 minutes.

Serves 2 to 4

Centre Pesto and mozzarella sub

Corn on the cob with chipotle butter

Corn on the cob goes with almost every picnic or barbecue dinner and this corn is no exception. If the chipotle butter is too hot for your palate, try a little garlic butter instead. Make it by combining melted butter and crushed garlic.

100 g unsalted butter

1½ tbsp canned chipotle chillies in adobo sauce, deseeded and finely chopped

1 tbsp fresh lime juice

¼ tsp sea salt

8 cobs fresh corn, husked

8 lime wedges

1 Melt the butter in a saucepan over medium heat. Add the chilli, lime juice and salt. Reduce the heat to low and cook for 1 minute, just to blend the flavours. Place the corn in a dish and brush each cob all over with the butter. Cover and refrigerate.

2 Grill the corn over medium-hot heat, turning frequently, cooking until the corn becomes darkened in spots, about 6 to 7 minutes. Serve warm with a lime wedge.

Serves 8

Asparagus spears with saffron aïoli

This vegetable dish is very versatile – it goes with any type of meal, whether it's grilled, barbecued or roasted. I especially like it with juicy and succulent prime rib of beef.

FOR THE AÏOLI

50 ml/¼ cup red wine vinegar

1 tbsp golden syrup

Large pinch saffron threads

225 ml/1 cup mayonnaise

2 to 4 cloves garlic, crushed

Salt and pepper, to taste

FOR THE ASPARAGUS

900 g asparagus, trimmed

50 ml/¼ cup olive oil

50 g diced red pepper

1 Whisk the vinegar, golden syrup and saffron threads in a saucepan over medium-hot heat. Bring to the boil. Remove from the heat and allow to cool completely.

2 Mix the mayonnaise and garlic (to taste) in a bowl and blend well. Add the cooled saffron mixture. Season to taste with salt and pepper. Cover and refrigerate until needed.

3 Place the asparagus spears in a glass baking dish. Pour the oil over the asparagus and toss to coat. Grill over medium-hot heat, turning as needed, until tender-crisp, about 4 to 5 minutes. Transfer to a serving platter, garnish with diced red pepper and sea salt. Serve with the aïoli.

Serves 6 to 8

Opposite Asparagus spears with saffron aioli

Polenta with black bean salsa

This is a hybrid dish, combining Italian polenta with black bean salsa. Serve it for lunch or a light dinner, but remember - the polenta must be prepared in advance. Traditional polenta - a coarse grind of cornmeal similar to grits - needs cooking for at least 30 minutes.

1.4 l/6 cups water

2 tsp salt

270 g polenta

Olive oil

350 g Cheddar cheese, sliced thinly

350 ml/1½ cups black bean salsa (see page 144)

1 To make the polenta, lightly oil a loaf tin. Bring the water and salt to the boil in a large saucepan. Slowly add the polenta, stirring constantly and watching for lumps.

2 Reduce the heat to low and cook, stirring almost constantly, until the polenta forms a thick mass that pulls cleanly away from the sides of the pan, about 30 minutes.

3 Pour the polenta into the loaf tin and smooth the top. Let it cool for at least 30 minutes before turning out.

4 Cut the polenta into slices about 4 cm thick. To grill, lightly brush the cut edges with the oil. Grill over high heat until the bottom is charred with grill marks, about 3 minutes. Turn the polenta, put a slice of cheese on top and cook until that side is charred with grill marks, about 3 minutes.

5 Transfer the polenta to a serving plate. Spoon the black bean salsa over the top and serve.

Serves 6

Polenta with corn salad

If you like cornbread, then you're sure to love polenta - think of it as "gourmet cornbread".

FOR THE POLENTA

900 ml/4 cups water

1 tsp sea salt

150 g polenta (or yellow cornmeal)

40 g grated Parmesan

Olive oil

FOR THE SALAD

50 ml/¼ cup olive oil

3 tbsp fresh lime juice

2 cloves garlic, crushed

4 cobs fresh corn, husked

1 large red onion, cut into 1-cm thick slices

Olive oil

550 ml/2½ cups deseeded and chopped tomatoes

200 g cucumber, chopped

2 tbsp finely chopped mint

Salt and pepper, to taste

1 Bring the water and salt to the boil in a large saucepan. Gradually whisk in the polenta until the mixture is boiling and smooth in texture. Reduce the heat to low. Cook until very thick, whisking often, about 25 minutes (use less time for yellow cornmeal). Whisk in the cheese. Lightly oil an 20 x 20 x 5-cm glass baking dish or tin. Spread the mixture in the dish or tin and cool slightly. Cover and chill at least 6 hours, or overnight.

2 For the salad, whisk the oil, lime juice and garlic in a small bowl until blended. Cover and set aside.

3 Brush the corn cobs and onion slices with olive oil and grill over medium heat, turning often, until slightly charred and tender - about 8 to 10 minutes for the corn and 12 to 14 minutes for the onions. Leave to cool. Cut the kernels off the corn cobs and chop the onions. Combine the corn and onions with the tomatoes, cucumbers and mint in a large bowl. Whisk the dressing again and add it to the vegetables. Toss and season to taste with salt and pepper. Cover and refrigerate.

4 Cut the polenta into four squares and then cut each square into two triangles. Brush the polenta with olive oil and grill under a medium heat for about 4 to 5 minutes per side. Divide the salad on to plates and serve with the polenta on the side.

Serves 4

SAUCES AND SALSAS 7

Above left *The* ultimate barbecue sauce **right** Horseradish-mustard cream

The ultimate barbecue sauce

Use this sauce as a glaze if you wish. Brush it over food around the end of the barbecuing process, but take care that it does not burn.

1 tbsp olive oil
1 large onion, chopped finely
3 cloves garlic, chopped finely
300 ml/1¼ cups stout beer
6 tbsp ketchup
4 tbsp tomato purée
4 tbsp Worcestershire sauce
2 tbsp malt vinegar
2 tbsp packed brown sugar
2 tbsp Dijon mustard
½ tsp freshly ground black pepper

1 Heat the oil in a large saucepan and add the onion and garlic. Cook over medium heat, stirring frequently, until the onion is soft but not brown, about 5 minutes.

2 Add the remaining ingredients and stir well.

3 Bring to the boil, cover and simmer gently, stirring occasionally for 15 to 20 minutes. If the sauce needs thickening, remove the lid and simmer for another 10 minutes until the sauce reaches the desired consistency.

Makes 350 ml/1½ cups

Horseradish-mustard cream

This sauce is good on all meats and some poultry, particularly beef and duck. As a healthier alternative, use yoghurt instead of the soured cream.

3 tbsp wholegrain mustard
2 tbsp grated fresh horseradish or horseradish sauce
1 tsp honey
225 ml/1 cup soured cream
2 tbsp snipped chives

Mix the mustard and horseradish with the honey. Stir in the soured cream and chives. Refrigerate for at least an hour, then leave at room temperature for 30 minutes before using.

Makes 300 ml/1¼ cups

Treacle barbecue sauce

This barbecue sauce relies on treacle for a thicker, richer and deeper barbecue flavour. Besides being great with meats, it's also wonderful used to make baked beans.

Generous 125 ml/½ cup treacle
Generous 125 ml/½ cup cider vinegar
Scant 125 ml/½ cup groundnut oil
4 tbsp Worcestershire sauce
½ tsp Tabasco sauce
1 tbsp paprika
1 tsp chilli powder
1 tsp dried mustard
1 crumbled bay leaf
1 tsp garlic powder
½ tsp celery salt

Thin the treacle by warming it gently in a medium saucepan. Add the remaining ingredients and mix well.

Makes 350 ml/1½ cups

Aïoli

Aioli seems like a gourmet item thanks to its popularity in restaurants, but it's so simple to make, you'll wonder why you haven't done it sooner. It tastes great as a dip not only for grilled items, but for almost any food, cooked or raw.

1 large egg
1 clove garlic
Juice of ½ lemon

1 tsp dried mustard
Cayenne pepper, to taste
225 ml/1 cup olive oil

1 Blend all the ingredients, except the oil, in a blender or food processor.

2 With the blender running, add the olive oil in a continuous stream until the mixture starts to emulsify. Continue adding the oil in a thin stream until the mixture thickens and all the oil has been used up.

Makes 1¼ cups

Right Aïoli

Salmoriglio

In Sicily, salmoriglio is used as *the* marinade for fish that is to be grilled, usually threaded onto skewers. Sicilians believe that the only way to make a really good salmoriglio is to add seawater; in the absence of this ingredient, use sea salt.

1 clove garlic

1 tbsp finely chopped parsley

1½ tsp chopped fresh oregano

1 tsp chopped fresh rosemary

175 ml/¾ cup olive oil, slightly warmed

3 tbsp hot water

4 tbsp fresh lemon juice

Sea salt and freshly ground pepper, to taste

1 Put the garlic, herbs and salt into a mortar or bowl and pound to a paste with a pestle or the end of a rolling pin.

2 Pour the oil into a warmed bowl. Using a fork or a whisk, slowly whisk in the hot water followed by the lemon juice until well emulsified. Add the herb and garlic mixture and the salt and pepper.

3 Put the bowl over a saucepan of hot water and warm for 5 minutes, whisking occasionally. Allow to cool before using.

Makes 300 ml/1¼ cups

Green chilli sauce

This delicious sauce is traditionally made with green New Mexico chillies. However, since they are hard to find year-round, you can substitute mild Anaheim chillies and several jalapeño or serrano chillies to boost the heat. This sauce is a key ingredient in enchiladas, but can also be served with tacos, chops and many other dishes.

6 green chillies, plus 3 to 4
  jalapeño or serrano chillies

3 cloves garlic

4 tomatoes, halved

1 onion, peeled and halved

¼ tsp sea salt

225 ml/1 cup water or
  chicken stock

1 Grill the chillies, garlic, tomatoes and onion in a tray directly over the coals until they are brown and blistered. Deseed the chillies and cut them into strips. Peel the garlic. Cut the tomatoes and onions into chunks.

2 Purée all the vegetables with the salt and 125 ml/½ cup water in a blender or food processor.

3 Put the purée in a medium saucepan with the remaining water and simmer until it reaches the desired consistency. Adjust the seasoning if necessary.

Makes about 450 ml/2 cups

Asian sweet-and-sour sauce

There are many different recipes for sweet-and-sour sauce. This one is particularly delicious with burgers, chops and ribs. It is so easy to prepare and can be made quickly, especially if you use canned tomatoes.

1 tbsp olive oil

1 onion, sliced thinly

1 clove garlic, crushed

1 green pepper, deseeded
  and sliced thinly

One 1400-g can crushed
  tomatoes, or 450 g fresh
  tomatoes, skinned and
  chopped

4 tbsp packed brown sugar

1 tsp mixed dried herbs

6 tbsp water

225-g can pineapple chunks
  in juice

4 tbsp red wine vinegar

4 tbsp light soy sauce

2 tbsp cornflour

Sea salt and freshly ground
  pepper, to taste

1 Heat the oil in a saucepan and add the onion, garlic and pepper. Cook gently, stirring occasionally, until the vegetables are soft but not brown, about 5 minutes.

2 Stir in the tomatoes, sugar, herbs and water.

3 Drain the pineapple, adding the juice to the saucepan.

4 Whisk together the vinegar, soy sauce and cornflour, and add to the sauce.

5 Bring to the boil, stirring, until the sauce thickens and becomes glossy. Reduce heat and simmer gently for 5 minutes.

6 Season with the salt and pepper and add the pineapple chunks. Heat and serve.

Makes about 450ml/2 cups

Opposite Green chilli sauce

Béarnaise sauce

The tarragon in this sauce provides such a distinctive flavour that you really cannot substitute another herb.

6 sprigs tarragon and chervil, chopped

2 to 3 white peppercorns, crushed

1 tbsp chopped shallot

2 tbsp tarragon vinegar

Generous 50 ml/¼ cup dry white wine

3 large egg yolks

1 tbsp water

225 g unsalted butter, softened

A few drips of lemon juice

Sea salt, to taste

Pinch of cayenne pepper

1 Combine half the herbs, the peppercorns, shallots, vinegar and white wine in a saucepan. Bring to the boil and reduce the mixture to about 2 tablespoons.

2 Beat the egg yolks with the water and add to the reduced liquid. Place in the top of a double boiler containing hot, not boiling, water. Whisk until fluffy.

3 Add the butter, 1 tablespoon at a time, whisking until the sauce has thickened. Season with the lemon juice, salt and cayenne pepper. Serve warm.

Makes 225 ml/1 cup

Peppercorn sauce

This is a very pungent green peppercorn sauce. It can be made in advance and reheated just before serving.

1 tsp unsalted butter

1 tbsp peppercorn liquid (from the jar of peppercorns)

1½ tbsp cognac

2 tbsp white wine

2 tbsp canned green peppercorns, drained

350 ml/1½ cups beef stock

4 tbsp soured cream

1 Combine the butter, peppercorn liquid, cognac and wine in a saucepan. Bring to the boil, reduce the heat and simmer until reduced to 1 tablespoon.

2 Add the peppercorns and beef stock and reduce again to about 125 ml/½ cup.

3 Add the soured cream and salt, bring to the boil and serve with steaks.

Makes 350 ml/1½ cups

Onion raita

A refreshing salad to serve with fried dishes or with grilled steak. It is also a cooking accompaniment to many Indian dishes.

1 onion, sliced finely

2 tbsp vegetable oil

1 tsp cumin seeds

1 red onion, sliced finely

1 small red chilli, deseeded and chopped finely

2 to 3 tbsp chopped fresh coriander

350 ml/1½ cups plain yoghurt

Sea salt and freshly ground pepper, to taste

1 Heat the oil in a frying pan and cook the onion until softened but not browned, 3 to 4 minutes. Add the cumin seeds and cook for another 2 to 3 minutes until golden brown. Transfer to a serving bowl.

2 Add all the remaining ingredients. Allow to stand for 15 minutes before serving, if possible, to allow the flavours to blend.

Makes 450 ml/2 cups

Above left Peppercorn sauce **right** Onion raita

Mango and red pepper salsa

Spicy fruit salsas are especially good with grilled or broiled fish. Substitute pawpaw for the mangoes for an equally delicious salsa. For a milder but still somewhat spicy salsa, remove the veins and seeds from the chillies. For a very hot salsa, use one habenero or Scotch bonnet chilli (but protect yourself with gloves while handling) instead of one of the jalapeños.

2 ripe mangoes, peeled and diced

1 red pepper, deseeded and diced

1 to 2 jalapeño or Serrano chillies, finely chopped

2 cloves garlic, chopped

Juice of 1 lime

¼ to ½ red onion, chopped

4 tbsp chopped coriander

Sea salt, to taste

Combine all the ingredients in a medium bowl and mix well. Refrigerate until needed.

Makes 450 ml/2 cups

Black bean salsa

Black bean salsa is an excellent spicy relish, perfect with fish, chicken and burgers. To keep it simple, use canned beans and, remember, kidney beans are a good alternative if black beans are hard to find.

450-g can black beans, or kidney beans, drained and rinsed

75 g chopped red pepper

3 spring onions, chopped

2 red chillies, chopped finely

3 tbsp chopped coriander

1½ tsp chopped fresh oregano

1 tbsp olive oil

Juice of 1 lime

Sea salt and freshly ground black pepper

Combine all the ingredients. Leave to stand for at least 30 minutes for the flavours to develop. Taste and if necessary adjust the seasoning.

Makes 350 ml/1½ cups

Salsa cruda

This classic, chunky mixture of chillies and a few flavourings defines Mexican cuisine around the world. As a bonus, it is very healthy as well and is best made and eaten on the same day.

3 to 5 jalapeño chillies, chopped finely

1 mild green chilli

3 spring onions (white and green parts), chopped finely

5 cloves garlic, crushed

3 to 5 tomatoes, diced

Pinch of sugar

¼ tsp cumin, or more to taste

Sea salt, to taste

5 to 6 tbsp chopped fresh coriander

Juice of ½ lemon or lime

1 Combine the chillies with the spring onions, garlic and tomato, and then season with the sugar, cumin and salt.

2 Toss with the coriander and lemon juice. Add more salt and cumin if necessary. Serve immediately or refrigerate until ready to use.

Makes 175 ml/³⁄₄ cup

Opposite Mango and red pepper salsa

Onion and chilli salsa

Grilling brings out a different side in a chilli, as it does with onions and garlic. It mellows these ingredients and draws out their sweetness, giving this salsa a completely different character than those that are made raw.

1 onion, unpeeled, cut in half

10 cloves garlic, whole and unpeeled

3 medium-hot chillies, such as jalapeño, whole

1 green pepper, cut in half

Sea salt, to taste

Juice of ½ to 1 lemon, or to taste

1 Grill the onion, garlic, chillies and green pepper over medium-hot heat, covered, turning once, until charred on both sides, 10 to 15 minutes. Remove from the heat and place in a paper bag to cool.

2 When cool enough to handle, remove their skins and stems (remove the seeds from the chillies) and chop. Combine all the ingredients in a medium bowl. Season with the salt and lemon juice.

Makes 225 ml/1 cup

Mango, pawpaw and chilli relish

Serve this relish as a side dish with rich barbecued foods, rice and curries. The mango and pawpaw must be under-ripe.

2 under-ripe green mangoes, peeled and sliced thinly

1 under-ripe green pawpaw, peeled and sliced thinly

2 to 3 assorted red chillies, sliced thinly

Sugar, to taste

Sea salt, to taste

Serve the sliced mango and pawpaw sprinkled with half the chillies and let each diner sprinkle the sugar, salt and additional chillies to his or her taste.

Makes 450 ml/2 cups

Opposite Mango, pawpaw and chilli relish

Spicy avocado and red pepper dip

The chilli and red pepper used in this recipe give a mild taste. For those who enjoy a stronger flavour, adjust accordingly.

1 large avocado, stoned and chopped

1 tsp fresh lemon juice

1 red pepper, chopped finely

1 spring onion (white and green parts), chopped finely

½ tsp ground coriander

¼ tsp chilli powder

2 tbsp plain yoghurt

Sea salt and freshly ground pepper, to taste

1 Mash the chopped avocado in a small bowl and sprinkle with the lemon juice.

2 Add the remaining ingredients and mix well.

Makes 350 ml/1½ cups

Hummus

This chick pea dip originates in the Middle East and may be eaten with bread or sliced fresh vegetables.

225 ml/1 cup chick peas, soaked overnight

2 to 3 cloves garlic

125 ml/½ cup tahini

75 ml/⅓ cup olive oil

Sea salt and freshly ground pepper, to taste

Juice of ½ lemon (optional)

Paprika

1 Rinse the chick peas under cold running water, then bring them to the boil in a saucepan of fresh water. Simmer for about 1½ hours until tender. Leave to cool, then drain, reserving some of the water.

2 Purée the chick peass, garlic, tahini and oil in a blender or food processor. Add as much reserved water as necessary to make a thick paste - about 150 ml/⅔ cup. Add salt, pepper and lemon juice if using.

3 Spoon the hummus into a serving dish and chill. Sprinkle with paprika just before serving.

Makes 225 ml/1 cup

SALADS AND BREADS 8

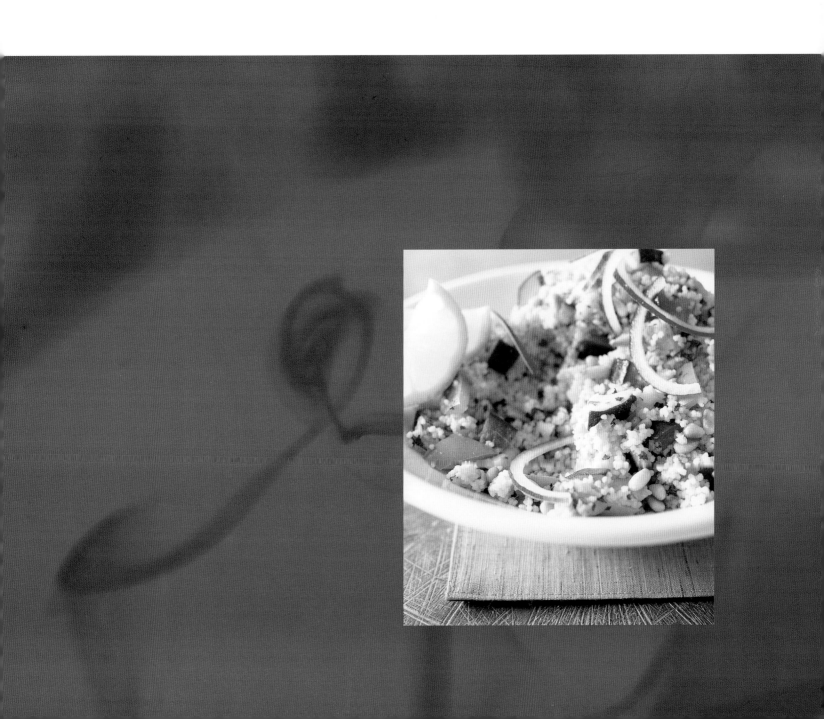

Andalusian chopped vegetable salad

When the weather is hot, make up large quantities of this salad and serve it chilled for any and every kind of meal - even breakfast, when it is exquisitely refreshing.

1 large cucumber, diced

3 to 5 small tomatoes, diced

1 carrot, diced

1 red pepper, diced

1 green pepper, diced (and yellow or orange pepper here, if desired)

1 small onion, chopped finely

3 to 5 cloves garlic, crushed

¼ tsp ground cumin or cumin seeds

Sea salt, to taste

Juice of 1 lemon

1 tsp sherry vinegar or white wine vinegar

3 tbsp olive oil

Combine the cucumber, tomato, carrot, peppers, onion and garlic in a medium bowl. Toss with the cumin, salt, lemon, sherry vinegar and oil. Taste for seasoning and chill until ready to eat.

Serves 4

Spiced couscous salad

Couscous should never be boiled. To prepare it, add boiling liquid to the grain, cover it and let it stand until fluffy.

1 small aubergine (eggplant)

1 small green pepper

1 small courgette (zucchini)

2 tbsp olive oil

1 onion, chopped

1 clove garlic, chopped

140 g uncooked couscous

225 ml/1 cup boiling chicken stock

1 tbsp toasted pine kernels

1 tbsp chopped fresh coriander

Sea salt and freshly ground pepper, to taste

1 red onion, thinly sliced, to garnish

1 Trim the aubergine, pepper and courgette. Cut the vegetables into 1-cm dice, keeping them separate from each other.

2 Heat the oil in a frying pan and cook the onion over medium heat until soft and transparent. Add the peppers, stir and cook for 3 minutes. Add the aubergine, stir and cook for 3 minutes, and then add the courgette and garlic and cook for another 3 minutes.

3 Stir in the uncooked couscous. Add the boiling chicken stock and bring the mixture back to the boil. Remove from the heat, cover and let the couscous rest off the heat for 10 minutes.

4 Add the pine kernels, coriander, salt and pepper. Serve garnished with thinly sliced red onion.

Serves 4

Opposite Spiced couscous salad

Sweet potato salad

This potato salad uses Indian flavours. If you like, use a mixture of half sweet potatoes and half baking potatoes.

2 medium sweet potatoes, peeled

4 tbsp olive oil

3 tbsp sesame oil

½ tsp cumin seeds

½ tsp coriander seeds

2 red onions, sliced thinly

2 cloves garlic, chopped finely

Juice of 2 limes

350 g canned chick peas

4 tbsp chopped coriander

Sesame seeds, toasted, to garnish

1 Cut the sweet potato into 1-cm dice. Place in a medium saucepan, cover with cold water and bring to the boil. Cook for 5 minutes. Drain, reserving the cooking liquid.

2 Heat the olive and sesame oils in a frying pan over medium-low heat and gently cook the cumin and coriander seeds. Add the sliced onions and cook until they soften and become translucent. Add the garlic and cook for another 2 minutes. Stir in the lime juice, increase the heat to high and cook for 1 to 2 minutes. Remove from the heat.

3 Gently fold the potatoes and chick peas into the onion mixture, add the coriander, toss gently and set aside for at least an hour before serving. Serve sprinkled with toasted sesame seeds as garnish.

Serves 4

Opposite Sweet potato salad

Minted carrot salad

As a substitute for the baby carrots, you may use full-size carrots that have been julienned. It will take a little more work to cut them up, but the results will be the same.

700 g baby carrots, washed

3 tbsp olive oil

3 tbsp long-grain rice

About 900 ml/4 cups chicken stock

Juice of 1 lemon

6 tbsp chopped fresh mint

Sea salt and freshly ground pepper, to taste

1 Slice the carrots in half lengthways. Heat the oil in a deep frying pan and cook the carrots over medium-low heat for 4 minutes.

2 Stir in the rice and the stock to cover by about 1 cm. Season with salt and pepper. Cover and simmer until all the liquid has been absorbed and the rice is fluffy.

3 Allow to cool slightly, then stir in the lemon juice and mint. Chill before serving.

Serves 4

Honey red cabbage

The combination of red cabbage, apples, vinegar and sugar is not really new, but this recipe includes honey, dill and garlic for a unique twist.

3 tbsp vegetable oil

1 large onion, sliced thinly

3 cloves garlic, crushed

1 medium red cabbage, shredded and chopped

2 sharp apples, quartered, cored and sliced thinly

2 tbsp white wine vinegar

1 tbsp sugar

2 tbsp fresh dill

50 ml/¼ cup honey

30 g sea salt

1 tsp freshly ground black pepper

1 Heat the oil in a large heavy frying pan. Add the onion and sauté until soft, about 3 to 4 minutes. Add the garlic and cook another minute. Stir in the cabbage and cook, covered, about 4 minutes or until the cabbage has wilted.

2 Add the apple, vinegar, sugar and dill. Stir well and continue to cook until the apples are tender, 7 to 8 minutes. Stir in the honey, salt and pepper, and cook for another 2 minutes.

Serves 6 to 8

Mixed bean salad

A good bean salad needs a tangy dressing to succeed. The garlic and lemon-based dressing provides a tasty complement to the texture of the salad.

100 g green beans, cut into halves

6 tbsp canned black-eyed beans

4 tbsp canned cannellini beans

4 tbsp canned red kidney beans

1 shallot, sliced

Sea salt and freshly ground pepper, to taste

FOR THE DRESSING

½ clove garlic, finely chopped

2 tbsp fresh lemon juice

1 tbsp sugar

4 tbsp chopped fresh parsley

2 medium tomatoes, sliced

A few black olives

1 Cook the green beans in a saucepan of boiling water 3 to 4 minutes. Drain and rinse well.

2 Put all the beans, the shallot, salt and pepper in a large bowl and mix well.

3 Combine the garlic, lemon juice, sugar and parsley in a jar and shake well.

4 Lay the sliced tomatoes on a serving plate, pile the bean mixture onto the centre and drizzle with the dressing. Garnish with the olives. Serve with crusty bread.

Serves 4

Opposite Mixed bean salad

Tomato and herb bruschetta

It doesn't matter if these little treats sit for a while once they have been put together. The tomato mixture soaks slightly into the toasted bread, with delightful results.

700 g tomatoes, preferably plum, peeled, seeded and chopped

2 cloves garlic, finely chopped

Sea salt and freshly ground pepper, to taste

1 tbsp balsamic vinegar

1 tbsp olive oil

1 tsp fresh lemon juice

6 slices crusty bread, cut into 1-cm thick slices

4 tbsp chopped fresh basil

1 Put the tomato, garlic, salt and pepper into a pan. Leave on the side of the grill to gently warm through.

2 Once the tomatoes are warm (not hot), stir in the vinegar, oil and lemon juice.

3 Toast the bread until golden brown on both sides. Place on to serving plates.

4 Stir the basil into the tomato mixture, pile on top of the bread slices and serve.

Serves 6

Grilled garlic bread

Everyone who likes garlic, loves garlic bread, so make sure you provide enough. It is a great standby to have on hand for people to enjoy while you are cooking the main course on the barbecue.

100 g slightly salted butter

3 cloves garlic, crushed

3 tbsp chopped fresh parsley

Freshly ground black pepper

1 French baguette

1 Soften the butter and blend in the garlic, parsley and some pepper.

2 Cut the bread diagonally into thick slices, cutting nearly but not quite all the way through. Spread the garlic butter on both sides of each slice and reassemble the loaf.

3 Wrap in thick foil and secure the seams. Grill over medium heat, turning occasionally, about 15 minutes until crisp and hot.

Serves 4

Opposite Tomato and herb bruschetta

Stuffed tomatoes

Tapas dishes are often gifts to vegetarians because many contain no meat. This dish is no exception. You can use small or large tomatoes for this recipe, which is a simple and colourful addition to any table.

8 small or 3 large tomatoes

4 hard-boiled eggs, cooled and peeled

175 ml/³/₄ cup aioli (see page 138), or garlic mayonnaise

Salt and freshly ground black pepper, to taste

1 tbsp chopped fresh parsley

1 tbsp fresh breadcrumbs (for large tomatoes)

Chopped fresh parsley

1 To peel the tomatoes, first cut an X-shaped incision at the top. Cover the tomatoes in boiling water for 10 seconds and then plunge them into a bowl of iced water for a few seconds. The skins should simply slip off.

2 Take a slice off the tops of the tomatoes and another slice off the base – just big enough to remove the rounded ends to keep the tomatoes sitting flat on the plate. Reserve the tops if using small tomatoes.

3 Mash the eggs with the mayonnaise, salt, pepper and parsley.

4 Fill the tomatoes, firmly pressing down the filling. With small tomatoes, replace the lids at a jaunty angle; if using big tomatoes, top with the breadcrumbs. Lightly brush the tomatoes with olive oil to prevent them from drying out.

Serves 4

Creole rice

The peppers, corn and tomatoes make this a colourful rice dish that can brighten up grilled meats.

4 tbsp unsalted butter

2 tbsp olive oil

1 small red onion, chopped finely

1 clove garlic

200 g long-grain rice

1 small green pepper, diced

425-g can chopped tomatoes

3 tbsp tomato purée

200-g can corn kernels

1 small bay leaf

Pinch of cayenne pepper

Sea salt and freshly ground pepper, to taste

450 ml/2 cups chicken stock

150 ml/²/₃ cup dry white wine

1 Heat the butter and oil in a frying pan and sauté the onion and garlic until the onion is soft and transparent. Remove the garlic clove and add the rice, stirring to coat, and continue stirring until the rice is transparent.

2 Stir in the pepper, tomato, tomato purée, corn, bay leaf, cayenne pepper, salt and pepper.

3 Bring the chicken stock and white wine to the boil in a medium saucepan and pour over the rice. Stir once, cover and simmer over low heat 10 to 15 minutes. Remove from the heat, take out the bay leaf and serve.

Serves 4 to 6

Opposite Creole rice

Pasta salad with caramelised onions, olives and walnuts

The onions are cooked very, very slowly so that they become meltingly sweet and gooey. Then they are simply combined with pasta, black olives and walnuts, which are added just before serving.

3 tbsp olive oil

2 large onions, sliced very thinly

2 tsp sugar

1½ tbsp tarragon, cider or white wine vinegar

225 g pasta, such as penne

100 g stoned black olives, halved

100 g walnut halves, lightly toasted and chopped

1 Heat the oil in a large frying pan and add the onions and sugar. Cook over low heat, stirring occasionally, until the onions are very soft, sweet and a rich golden-brown colour, 30 to 40 minutes. Leave to cool about 10 minutes, then stir in the vinegar.

2 Meanwhile, cook the pasta in a large pan of boiling, salted water until tender but still firm (*al dente*). Drain well and transfer to a large bowl. Add the onions, scraping any juices and brown bits from the bottom of the pan. Toss lightly. Cover and set aside until ready to use.

3 Just before serving, gently stir the olives and the walnuts into the pasta. Serve at room temperature.

Serves 6

Fried noodle salad

While this salad isn't exactly low in calories, it features a light dressing that is intensely flavourful. You may omit the omelette if you wish.

225 g Chinese rice noodles

1 tbsp caster sugar

1 tbsp light soy sauce

1 tbsp mirin (sweet rice wine)

2 tbsp groundnut oil

2 tbsp finely chopped shallots

1 clove garlic, crushed

225 g fresh beansprouts

1 tbsp fish sauce

2 tbsp fresh lemon juice

6 green chillies, deseeded and sliced finely

6 spring onions (green and white parts), chopped

3-egg omelette, cooled and cut into strips

1 bunch coriander, chopped

1 Cover the noodles with boiling water and leave to stand 1 minute. Drain and leave to dry. Combine the sugar, soy sauce and mirin in a small bowl and set aside.

2 Heat the oil in a deep frying pan or wok. Fry the noodles, a little at a time, until golden. Lift them out and drain on kitchen paper. Gently sauté the shallots and garlic, then drain and set aside with the noodles.

3 Combine the noodles, beansprouts, fish sauce, lemon juice, chillies and spring onions in a large bowl. Toss well. Garnish with the omelette strips and coriander.

Serves 4

Opposite Pasta salad with caramelised onions, olives and walnuts

Classic coleslaw

What barbecue party would be complete without a large bowl of creamy coleslaw? It is easy to make, yet impressive, too. For a change of pace, try replacing half the mayonnaise with yoghurt or soured cream.

1 large white cabbage, sliced finely

1 large carrot, grated

1 large onion, chopped finely

3 tbsp chopped fresh parsley

4 celery stalks, sliced thinly

250 ml/1 cup mayonnaise

Sea salt and freshly ground pepper, to taste

1 Put the cabbage, carrot, onion, parsley and celery into a large bowl and toss to mix.

2 Season the mayonnaise with salt and pepper and pour into the vegetable mixture. Toss until evenly coated.

3 Cover and chill 2 to 3 hours to allow the flavours to blend. Remove from the refrigerator about 30 minutes before serving. Serve at room temperature.

Serves 8

Gado gado

This traditional Indonesian salad combines raw and cooked vegetables. Here, cubes of tofu are part of the peanut and coconut dressing.

FOR THE PEANUT DRESSING

1 tsp lemongrass purée

1 clove garlic, crushed

1 tsp chilli sauce

2 tbsp vegetable oil

100 g crunchy peanut butter

175 ml/³/₄ cup coconut milk

Juice of 1 lime

2 tsp packed brown sugar

2 tsp sweet soy sauce

250 g firm tofu, cut into small cubes

FOR THE SALAD

225 g diced sweet potato

2 medium carrots, peeled and sliced thinly

50 g green beans, cut into 1-cm lengths

¹/₂ cucumber, sliced

2 pineapple rings, cut into small pieces

50 g bean sprouts

50 g Chinese leaves, sliced thinly

Chopped red chilli

1 For the dressing, place all the dressing ingredients except the tofu in a bowl and beat until smooth. Stir in the tofu and leave to stand at least one hour.

2 To make the salad, cook the sweet potato and carrot in a pan of boiling water for 5 minutes or until tender. Drain and refresh in cold water. Pat dry with kitchen paper.

3 Blanch the beans in a pan of boiling water for 1 minute, drain, refresh and pat dry with kitchen paper. Mix the cooked vegetables with the cucumber, pineapple pieces, beansprouts and shredded Chinese leaves. Pile the vegetable mixture in a serving dish. Spoon the peanut and tofu dressing over the salad and garnish with the chopped chilli.

Serves 4

DESSERTS 9

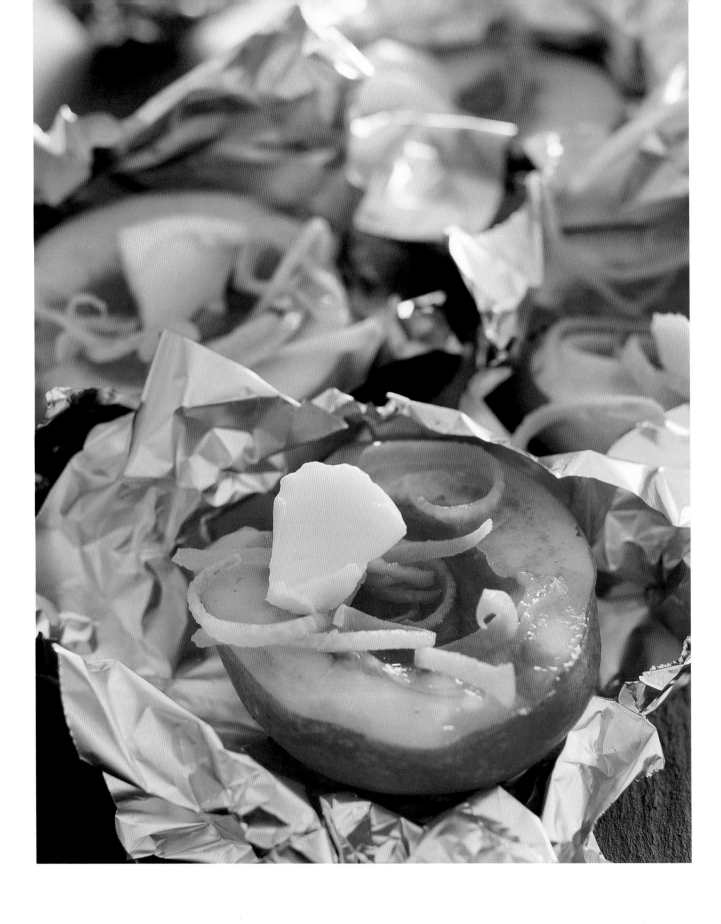

Nectarines with orange and almond butter

There is something very special about combining nectarines and almonds. The two flavours are a match made in heaven.

3 ripe nectarines

1 large orange

Boiling water

¼ tsp almond extract

50 g unsalted butter, cut
  into 6 pieces

225 ml/1 cup whipped cream
  or yoghurt

6 almond-flavored biscuits,
  crushed

1 Halve the nectarines and remove their stones. Lay each half, cut side up, on a large square of thick foil.

2 Using a vegetable peeler, pare the rind from half the orange and cut the rind into very thin strips. Pour boiling water over the strips and leave to stand for 10 minutes.

3 In a separate bowl, squeeze the juice from the orange and stir in the almond extract.

4 Into each nectarine half, put some of the orange juice, a piece of butter and some drained strips of orange rind. Close the foil parcel, being sure to secure the seams.

5 Grill the parcels, seam side up, over medium heat until the fruit has softened slightly and is warmed through, and the butter has melted, about 10 minutes.

6 Open the parcels and top the fruit with whipped cream and the crushed biscuits.

Serves 6

Summer fruit packets

Fresh mint adds a wonderful depth of flavour to fruit, especially when the flavour is enhanced with sugar and citrus. Next time you make a fruit salad, add some finely chopped fresh mint for a little extra zing.

2 peaches

Boiling water

225 g strawberries, hulled
  and washed

225 g cherries, stoned

2 kiwi fruit, peeled and
  sliced

50 g unsalted butter

2 tbsp packed brown sugar

Grated rind and juice of
  1 orange

4 sprigs fresh mint

1 Place the peaches in a bowl and pour boiling water over them. Leave to stand 1 minute, then drain and peel. Cut the peaches in half, remove their stones and slice.

2 Put the strawberries and cherries in a large bowl and add the sliced peaches and kiwi fruit. Gently mix.

3 Cut four large squares of heavy-duty foil. Divide the fruit between the squares.

4 Heat the butter, sugar, orange rind and orange juice over medium heat in a small saucepan until the sugar has melted. Spoon this mixture over the fruit and top each portion with a sprig of mint. Close the parcels, being sure to secure the seams.

5 Grill the parcels over medium heat for about 10 minutes. Serve with whipped cream or ice cream.

Serves 4

Opposite Nectarines with orange and almond butter

Black bananas with butterscotch sauce

Banana skins are used as natural cooking wrappers in this dessert, and they are served with a uniquely decadent sauce.

50 g unsalted butter

75 g packed brown sugar

6 tbsp maple syrup

175 ml/³⁄₄ cup double cream

¹⁄₂ tsp vanilla extract

4 large bananas

1 Put the butter, brown sugar and maple syrup in a saucepan and heat slowly over the grill until the butter has just melted. Stir in the cream and vanilla extract. Move to the edge of the barbecue to keep warm.

2 Grill the unpeeled bananas over medium heat, turning once or twice, until black all over, about 15 minutes.

3 Lift the bananas on to a plate. Make a slit along each one and carefully pull the skin back.

4 Drizzle each banana with some sauce and serve the remainder on the side.

Serves 4

Texas Hill Country peach cobbler

Texas "Hill Country" is famous not only for its barbecue but also for its hot-out-of-the-oven peach cobbler. It is especially good topped with a scoop of homemade vanilla ice cream.

120 g plain flour

2 tsp baking powder

1 tsp ground cinnamon

¹⁄₂ tsp allspice

¹⁄₄ tsp salt

400 g sugar

175 ml/³⁄₄ cup milk

1 tbsp fresh lemon juice

100 g butter

400 g sliced fresh peaches

1 Preheat the oven to 180°C/350°F/Gas Mark 4. Sieve together the flour, baking powder, cinnamon and allspice. Mix in 350 g of the sugar. Slowly stir in the milk and then the lemon juice.

2 Melt the butter in a 23 x 23 x 5-cm baking tin. Pour the batter over the butter, but do not stir. Lay the peaches on top of the batter and sprinkle with the remaining sugar.

3 Bake in the oven for 1 hour or until a cocktail stick inserted in the centre comes out clean. Serve hot or cold.

Serves 6 to 8

Opposite Black bananas with butterscotch sauce

DESSERTS

Warm fruit and marshmallow kebabs with chocolate fondue

This is a fun dessert to produce at the end of a barbecue. Everyone dips into the chocolate sauce, and I guarantee there won't be any left over.

16 strawberries, washed and
  thoroughly dried

Wedge of watermelon, cut
  into 4-cm cubes

16 marshmallows

150 g plain chocolate

3 tbsp golden syrup

1 tbsp fresh lemon juice

8 small wooden skewers,
  soaked

1 Thread the pieces of fruit and marshmallows on to 8 small wooden skewers.

2 Put the chocolate, syrup and lemon juice in a flameproof dish. Heat gently on the grill, stirring frequently until the mixture is melted, glossy and smooth. Move to the edge of the grill and keep warm.

3 Cook the kebabs over medium heat for a few minutes, turning once, until just warmed through. The marshmallows will melt very quickly. An alternative is to skewer and grill the marshmallows separately, giving them just a flash over the fire to char.

4 Serve immediately with the chocolate sauce for dipping the kebabs, fondue style.

Serves 4

Centre Warm fruit and marshmallow kebabs with chocolate fondue

Hot fruit kebabs with maple cream

If you haven't served kebabs as the main course, now is your chance to conclude the meal with them. You can't lose with this combination of apple, lychees, banana and fig – it's wonderful!

300 ml/1¼ cups double cream

1 tbsp maple syrup

1 red apple, cored and cut into 6 wedges

2 bananas, peeled and sliced thickly

12 fresh lychees, peeled and stones removed

3 fresh plump figs, quartered

2 tbsp honey

2 tbsp unsalted butter, melted

6 small metal skewers or bamboo skewers, soaked

1 Put the cream and maple syrup into a bowl and whip lightly to form soft peaks. Cover and chill.

2 Thread the fruit on to six skewers. Stir the honey into the melted butter and brush over the kebabs.

3 Grill the kebabs over medium-high heat, turning frequently and brushing with any remaining honey mixture, until the fruit is slightly scorched and heated through, about 10 minutes.

4 Serve immediately with the maple cream.

Serves 6

Fresh strawberry pie

This was my grandfather's favourite summer dessert. Make it at the peak of the strawberry season, when the strawberries are at their sweetest.

FOR THE CRUST

150 g plain flour

100 g margarine

3 tbsp icing sugar

1 tsp vanilla extract

FOR THE FILLING

225 ml/1 cup water

225 g sugar

½ tsp salt

3 tbsp cornflour

125 ml/½ cup water

75-g pack strawberry jelly

FOR THE TOPPING

225 to 450 g hulled and halved strawberries

225 ml/1 cup double cream

2 tbsp icing sugar

1 tsp vanilla extract

1 Preheat the oven to 180°C/350°F/Gas Mark 4. Make the piecrust by combining the flour, sugar and vanilla and cutting in the margarine, until the mixture resembles breadcrumbs and forms into a dough. Press the dough into a 23-cm pie tin. Place baking parchment over the shell and cover with pie weights or dried beans. Bake for 15 to 20 minutes until lightly browned. Remove from the oven and cool.

2 For the filling, combine the water, sugar and salt in a pan. Bring to the boil. Combine the cornflour and 125 ml/½ cup water in a small bowl, stirring to make a paste. While constantly stirring, add the paste to the sugar-water mixture. Boil gently until clear and thick. Stir in the jelly, remove from the heat and cool.

3 Arrange the strawberries in the pie shell and carefully pour the cooled mixture over the berries. Chill for several hours.

4 Whip the double cream and add the sugar and vanilla. Spoon small dollops of whipped cream around the crust of the pie and serve.

Serves 6 to 8

Watermelon wedges with mango-berry salsa

This is an easy "throw it together" dessert that your friends will ask you to make again and again. It's low in calories yet deliciously sweet.

Twelve 4-cm thick watermelon wedges

400 g chopped mango

100 g fresh strawberries, hulled and chopped

1 tbsp finely chopped jalapeño chilli

2 tbsp finely chopped fresh mint

2 tbsp honey

1 Combine all the ingredients except the watermelon in a medium bowl. Refrigerate the salsa and watermelon until chilled.

2 To serve, spoon the mango salsa over the watermelon wedges.

Serves 6 to 12

Opposite Watermelon wedges with mango-berry salsa

Toasted spice cake with warm berries

Use any mix of berries you like in this dessert, or just one if you prefer; it will have a wonderful taste whatever you choose.

1 tsp mixed spice

100 g unsalted butter, melted

6 slices of Madeira cake, each about 1-inch thick

700 g mixed berries, such as blackberries, raspberries, blueberries

2 tbsp apple juice

2 tbsp sugar

2 tbsp Crème de cassis

1 Stir the mixed spice into the butter and lightly brush it over both sides of the cake slices.

2 Put the berries into a pan with the apple juice and sugar. Cook gently over the grill until the sugar dissolves and the juices begin to run from the fruit. Move the pan to a cool area of the grill and stir in the liqueur.

3 Warm the cake over medium heat, 1 minute per side, or until lightly toasted. The cake will burn easily, so watch it closely.

4 Serve the toasted cake with the warm berries spooned over the top, along with some vanilla ice cream.

Serves 6

Centre Toasted spice cake with warm berries

Glazed pears

This dessert was inspired by a classic – pears poached in red wine. In this grill version, a syrup made with red wine is spooned over the pears before they are wrapped in foil and placed on the grill.

6 large, firm pears, peeled, cored and halved

Grated rind and juice of ½ lemon

4 tbsp maple syrup

1 tsp vanilla extract

4 tbsp red wine

3 tbsp chopped pistachios

1 Cut four squares of heavy-duty foil. Lay a pear half on to each square.

2 Combine the remaining ingredients except the pistachios in a small saucepan and heat to boiling. Remove from the heat and spoon the mixture over each pear. Close the parcels, being sure to secure the seams.

3 Grill the pears over medium heat until they are hot and tender but firm, 5 to 8 minutes.

4 Open each packet and brush or spoon the juices from the packet back over the fruit. Sprinkle a few chopped pistachio nuts over each portion and serve.

Serves 4

Pecan squares

Pecan squares, along with pecan pies, are traditional barbecue fare. These squares are a variation on that theme and will complement all your favourite grilled dishes.

300 g unsalted butter, chilled and cut into pieces

50 g icing sugar

Pinch of salt

225 g plain flour

1 large egg, beaten

350 g packed light brown sugar

175 ml/³/₄ cup golden syrup

1½ tbsp vanilla extract

450 g pecan halves

1 Preheat oven to 190°C/375°F/Gas Mark 5.

2 Combine half the butter, the icing sugar and salt in a food processor. Process until you begin to see moist clumps. Add the flour and beaten egg and process just until a dough forms.

3 Press the dough into the bottom and about 2 cm up the sides, of a 23 x 33 x 5-cm baking tin. Bake until the crust is golden brown, about 20 to 25 minutes. Remove and cool slightly, but do not turn off the oven.

4 Bring the remaining half of the butter, the brown sugar and golden syrup to the boil in a heavy saucepan, stirring frequently. Boil for 2 minutes. Add the vanilla and stir in the pecans. Remove from the heat and pour the pecan mixture into the prepared crust. Bake until the filling sets and bubbles, about 25 minutes. Remove and cool completely on a wire rack. To serve, cut into 5-cm squares.

Makes about 24

Glazed pineapple with coconut rum

Strictly for the grown-ups! Make sure the children are safely occupied elsewhere when you serve up this decadent dessert.

1 small pineapple, skin and core removed and cut into 2.5 cm slices

85 g butter, melted

Icing sugar to taste

250 ml/1 cup double cream

2 tsp coconut liqueur

2 tsp dark rum

1 Brush the pineapple on all sides with the melted butter. Lightly dust with icing sugar.

2 Put the cream into a bowl and stir in icing sugar to taste. Add the liqueur and rum Lightly whip. the cream to smooth peaks. Cover and chill until required.

3 Cook the pineapple over a medium heat for 2 to 3 minutes on each side, until glazed and slightly scorched. Serve with the flavoured rum.

Serves 4